- Descriptions in this manua. at the time of writing this guide, and it may not be 100% accurate again if there is a major software update to iPhone 11, iPhone 11 Pro, or iPhone 11 Pro Max.

- Depending on your local network service provider or your region, some of the features discussed in this guide may not be available on your iPhone 11, iPhone 11 Pro, or iPhone 11 Pro Max.

- All information supplied in this guide is for an educational purpose only and users bear the responsibility for using it.

- The fonts contained in some of the screenshots used in this book have been boldened and enlarged to make it easier to see. You can also bolden or increase the font of your phone by going to **Settings** > **Display & Brightness** > **Text Size/Bold Text**. To adjust the text size, drag the slider on the **Text Size** screen. You would see the preview of the text size at the upper part of the screen. To embolden the font on your phone, tap **Bold Text**.

- Although I took tremendous effort to ensure that all information provided in this guide is correct, I will welcome your suggestions if you find out that any information provided in this guide is inadequate or you find a better way of doing some of the actions mentioned in this guide. All correspondences should be sent to pharmibrahimguides@gmail.com

About This Guide

Finally, a simplified guide on iPhone 11, iPhone 11 Pro, and iPhone 11 Pro Max is here– this guide is indeed a splendid companion for these high-end phones.

This is a comprehensive and no-nonsense guide, useful for both experts and newbies. This guide contains a lot of vital information on iPhone 11, iPhone 11 Pro and iPhone 11 Pro Max.

It is full of actionable steps, hints, notes, screenshots, and suggestions. This guide is specifically written for newbies/beginners and seniors; nonetheless, I firmly believe that even the tech-savvy among us will derive some benefits from reading it.

Enjoy yourself as you go through this very comprehensive guide.

PS: Please make sure you do not give the gift of iPhone 11, iPhone 11 Pro, or iPhone 11 Pro Max without giving this companion guide alongside with it. This guide makes your gift a complete one.

Table of Contents

How to Use This Guide (Please Read!)

This guide is an unofficial manual of iPhone 11, iPhone 11 Pro, and iPhone 11 Pro Max, and it should be used just as you use any reference book or manual.

To quickly find a topic, please use the table of contents or index. This will allow you to find information quickly and save time.

When I say you should carry out a set of tasks, for example when I say you should tap **Settings >Do Not Disturb> Always**, what I mean is that you should tap on **Settings** and then tap on **Do Not Disturb**. And lastly, you should tap on **Always**.

When a function is enabled, the status switch will appear bold and colored. On the other hand, when a function is disabled, the status switch will appear gray.

4:51

‹ Settings   **Do Not Disturb**

Do Not Disturb

Do Not Disturb silences calls and
notifications.

Scheduled   **Enabled function**

From   10:00 PM
To   7:00 AM

Dim Lock Screen   **Disabled function**

Scheduled turns on Do Not Disturb for the
time period you select. Dim Lock Screen
darkens the lock screen and sends
notifications to Notification Center during
that time.

SILENCE:

Always

While iPhone is Locked   ✓

Incoming calls and notifications will be
silenced while iPhone is locked.

PHONE

I hope this guide helps you get the most out of your iPhone

Getting Started With Your iPhone

Unpacking Your Device

When you unpack your product box, check your product box for the
following items:

1. iPhone 11, iPhone 11 Pro, or iPhone 11 Pro Max
2. EarPods with Lightning Connector
3. Lightning to USB cable
4. USB Power Adapter
5. Eject Pin (the eject pin is located on one of the quick start
   guides)
6. Quick Start Guides

Inserting a SIM Card

1. While the phone is off, insert the SIM ejection tool into the
   SIM tray eject hole and push until the tray pops out. Please
   note that you may need to apply force for the SIM tray to pop
   out. The SIM ejection tool is included in the iPhone's box.
   The eject hole is the small hole located below the side key.
2. Place the SIM Card on the tray with the metal contacts facing
   down.
3. Insert the SIM Card tray into the phone and push until it
   locks into place
4. Press and hold the Side Button to turn the phone on.

Please note that iPhone 11, iPhone 11 Pro, or iPhone 11 Pro Max uses a Nano-SIM Card. Besides, you may not need to turn off your phone before you remove the SIM Card.

Turning Your Phone on and off

Just like many other smartphones, turning on your device is as simple as ABC. To turn on your phone, press and hold the Side button. If you are turning on your phone for the first time, carefully follow the on-screen instructions to set it up.

To turn off your phone, press and hold the side button and either volume button. Then drag the slider.

Please do not be annoyed if you find it unnecessary that how to on/off your device is included in this guide. I have included it in case some readers of this guide are novices and know close to nothing about smartphones.

Note: Please note that you will need your Apple ID to set up your device. If you are using an iPhone for the first time and you don't have an Apple ID, you may create one whenever you're asked to sign in by clicking the account-creation button.

Tips:

- Some network providers may require you to enter a PIN when you switch on your phone. You can try entering **0000 or 1234.** This is the default PIN for many network providers. If you have a problem entering the correct PIN, please contact your network service provider.

- During your phone setup, you may be able to skip some processes. Usually, you will have the option to perform these processes in the future by going to your phone settings.

- While using your phone for the first time, you should have the option to transfer contents from your old Android phone to iPhone 11, iPhone 11 Pro, or iPhone 11 Pro Max. Just carefully follow the onscreen instructions to do this. *Please note that if you skip this process during the setup, you may not be able to use this process of file transfer again unless you want to erase your iPhone (see page 231) and start over.* To learn more about this process of file transfer, please see page 14.

- It is likely that your phone will consume a large amount of data during the phone setup, I will recommend that you connect to a wireless network if you can. Using a mobile network during the setup might be expensive.
- When you start using your phone, you may probably notice that your phone screen locks within few seconds after you finish interacting with it. To make your phone stay longer before it locks, change the Auto-lock setting. To do this:

    o From the Home screen, tap the Settings icon .
    o Scroll down and tap **Display & Brightness**.
    o Tap on **Auto-Lock**. Then choose an option.

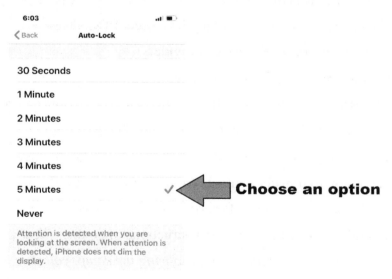

Please note that selecting a longer timeout may make your battery discharge faster. Also, note that you may be unable to change the lock time if *Low Power Mode* is enabled. To learn more about Low Power Mode, please go to page 9.

- *Do you need to charge your phone before first use?*

To the best of my knowledge, it is not compulsory. If you charge it before first use, that is cool. But if there is no way to charge it, then you can use it straight away without charging it. I have learned that the new lithium batteries used in smartphones don't really need to be charged before first use (provided that the battery still has power).

Get to Know the Settings Tab

I think it will be great to introduce you to the settings tab because I would be referring to this tab a lot.

The settings tab has many subsections, and because of this, I would recommend that you use the **Search** menu (denoted by the lens icon

Q) to find what you are looking for quickly. To access the

Settings menu, from the Home screen, tap **Settings** .

Then tap on the search bar (located at the top of the screen) and type a keyword corresponding to the settings you are looking for. For example, if you are looking for settings relating to battery, just type **Battery** into the search bar. The result filters as you type.

If the search bar is not showing, simply swipe down from the middle of the screen.

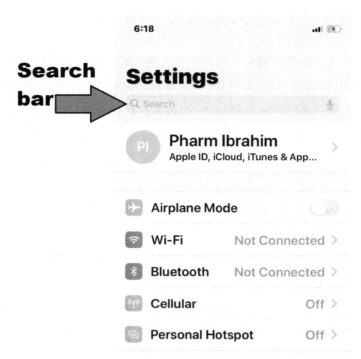

To dismiss the search bar, simply tap **Cancel** that appears next to the search bar.

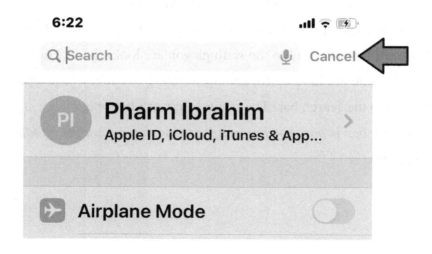

To use voice dictation, tap the microphone button  on the search bar. Enable the dictation if needed and then say a word or a phrase. For example, you may say **battery** if you want to search for settings relating to battery.

Searching Your Device/Dictionary

You can search for information on your device or search for a word in the dictionary.

To do this:

1. While on the Home screen, swipe down from the middle of the screen.
2. Tap the search field and type what you want to search for. The list filters as you type.

3. Tap a search result to open it.
4. To dismiss the search bar, swipe up the screen.

Tip: To change what is included in the search results, go to **Settings** 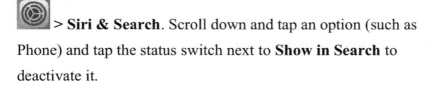 > **Siri & Search**. Scroll down and tap an option (such as Phone) and tap the status switch next to **Show in Search** to deactivate it.

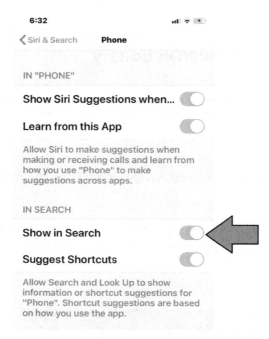

Charging Your Device

If you are using your iPhone 11, iPhone 11 Pro, or iPhone 11 Pro Max more often (especially if you use Wi-Fi more often), you may realize that you need to charge your phone every day. One of the best times to charge your device is when you are taking a shower as you are not likely to be using it this time.

To learn more about how to use your phone for a longer time on battery, please go to page 228.

To charge your iPhone 11, iPhone 11 Pro, or iPhone 11 Pro Max:

1. When you first open your product box, you will notice that the power cord consists of two parts (i.e. the **lightning to USB cable** and the **USB power adapter**), connect these two parts together.

2. Connect the other end of the **lightning to USB cable** or **USB-C to lightning cable** to the lightning port of your device, making sure that both the charging cable and the charging port on your device make good contact.

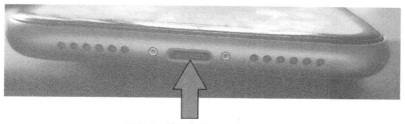

Lightning Port Connector

3. Plug the power cord to an electrical outlet. The charging time may be long if you are using your device while charging it.

Tip: To customize the battery options; from the Home screen, tap on

Settings 🔘 , and select **Battery.** To increase the number of hours you use your phone on battery, select **Low Power Mode**. Please note that *Low Power Mode* may affect the way your phone behaves.

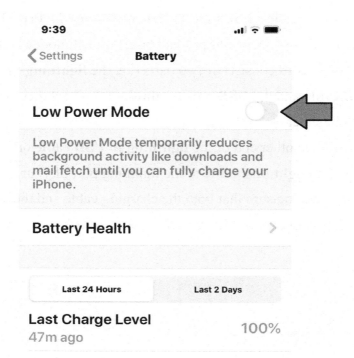

Note: *It is not advisable to use the lightning port while it is wet. If your phone has contact with water, please make sure you dry the lightning port before using it. Also, make sure the charging cord is free of water (or other liquid) before using it. Although your device is water-resistant, it is not advisable at all to charge it while the device is wet. This may cause electric shock or damage your device.*

Tip: You can view the battery percentage on your phone by swiping down from the top right-hand of the screen.

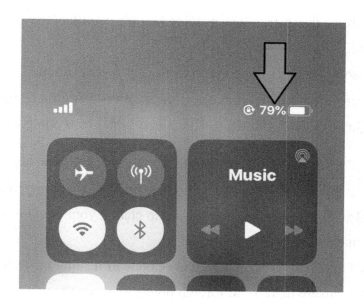

What About the Wireless Charging

iPhone 11, iPhone 11 Pro and iPhone 11 Pro Max have built-in wireless charging feature, and this means that you can charge the battery on your device using a wireless charger (sold separately).

To charge your device wirelessly:

- Using a USB cord, connect a power adapter to the wireless charger (sold separately) and then plug it to a wall socket. A wireless charger should come with a power adapter. iPhone 11, iPhone 11 Pro and iPhone 11 Pro Max work with Qi-certified chargers.

- If you are using your wireless charger for the first time, remove any protective nylon from the surface of the wireless charger. Then place your iPhone on the wireless charger following the instructions provided by the manufacturer of the wireless charger.

Please note that if you connect a charger to your mobile device during wireless charging, the wireless charging feature might be unavailable. *I will recommend you avoid doing so.*

In addition, depending on the type of the wireless charger you are using, charging wirelessly may take a longer time when compared to using a cable. This means that if you want to charge your device faster, you may consider using a cable.

Protection Tip: To avoid damaging your phone or heating up your phone, please ensure there is no foreign object between the wireless charger and your phone. Foreign objects include (but not limited to) metals, credit cards, and magnets.

What About the External Memory Card

As usual, the memories of iPhone 11, iPhone 11 Pro and iPhone 11 Pro Max are not expandable.

Maintaining the Water and Dust Resistance

Although iPhone 11, iPhone 11 Pro and iPhone 11 Pro Max are water and dust resistant, there are few things you still have to put at the back of your mind so that you don't spoil your phone. Some of those things you have to know are discussed below:

- Even though iPhone 11 is water-resistant, you can't still immerse the device in water deeper than 2m and/or keep it submerged for more than 30 minutes.

- On the other hand, you can't immerse iPhone 11 Pro or iPhone 11 Pro Max in water deeper than 4m and/or keep it submerged for more than 30 minutes.

- Apple has made it known that it won't cover liquid/water damage on the iPhone 11 or iPhone 11 Pro/Pro Max under the warranty. So, please be careful when using your phone under water.

- Splash, water, and dust resistance are not permanent conditions, and resistance might decrease because of normal wear.

- If your phone falls down from a considerable height, water and dust resistance properties might be affected.

- The screen of your device may not respond properly when it is wet. I will advise that you clean it with a dry towel to get the full functionality.

- It is not advisable to put your device under water moving with force such as tap water. This is because water may get into the inner part of your device in the process. In addition, do not expose the device to saltwater or ionized water.

- While your screen is wet, you may not enjoy using your device as you should. You may need to clean it with a dry towel to make it work properly.

- To avoid electric shock, please don't charge your device while it is wet or while it is under water.

- Make sure you close the SIM Card slot properly before you submerge your device in water.

Moving Your Items from Your Android Phone to Your iPhone 11, iPhone 11 Pro, or iPhone 11 Pro Max

The easiest way to transfer your items from your old phone (Android Phone) to your new iPhone 11, iPhone 11 Pro, or iPhone 11 Pro Max is through the use of **Move to iOS** app. To use this method, please follow the instructions below:

Please note that you can only use this method while setting up your new iOS device. If you have already set up your iPhone, this method may not work for you unless you want to erase your iPhone (see page 231) and start over. Also, you may need internet connections on your Android phone and iPhone to use this method.

- Download **Move to iOS** app to your Android phone from Google store. Open the app and tap **Continue**. Accept the terms and tap **Next**.

- While setting up your new iPhone, follow the onscreen prompts until you see **Apps & Data** screen. Tap **Move Data from Android,** and tap **Continue**. Then wait for a ten-digit or six-digit code to appear.

- On your Android device, enter the code. Then wait for the Transfer Data screen to appear. Select the content that you want to transfer and tap **Next.**
- When the transfer process is complete, tap **Continue Setting Up iPhone** to continue setting up your device.

Using the Touch Screen

Your phone touch screen allows you to easily select items or perform functions. With the touch screen, you may operate your phone like a pro.

Notes:

- Do not tap/press the touch screen with sharp tools. Doing so may damage the touch screen or cause it to malfunction.
- Do not allow the touch screen to come into contact with other electrical appliances. This may cause the touch screen to malfunction.
- When the touch screen is wet, endeavor to clean it with a dry towel before using it. The touchscreen may not function properly when wet.
- For optimal use of the screen, you may need to remove the screen protector before using it. However, good screen protector should be fully usable with your device.

You may control your touch screen with the following actions:

Tap: Touch once with your finger to select or launch a menu, application or option.

Tap and hold: Tap an item and hold it for more than a second to perform certain operations.

Tap and drag: Tap and drag with your finger, to move an item to a different location.

Pinch: Place two fingers far apart, and then draw them closer together to zoom out. Do the reverse to zoom in.

> **To Lock or Unlock the Touch Screen:**

When you do not use the device for a specified period, your device turns off the touch screen and automatically locks the touch screen so as to prevent any unwanted device operations and save battery. To adjust the automatic lock timing, go to **Settings**  > **Display & Brightness** > **Auto-Lock**.

You can also manually lock the touch screen by pressing the side button.

To unlock, turn on the screen by pressing the side button and then drag the slider from the bottom of the screen up. If you have already set a lock screen password, you will be prompted to enter a passcode.

Note: You can change the lock screen method on your phone, please refer to page 51.

Rotating the Touch Screen

Your phone has a built-in motion sensor that detects its orientation. If you rotate your device, the interface will automatically rotate according to the orientation.

➢ **To activate or deactivate screen rotation**

Swipe down from the top-right edge of the screen to access Action Center on your iPhone. Then tap [icon]. Please make sure you are swiping down from the upper right-hand side of the screen to get what you want.

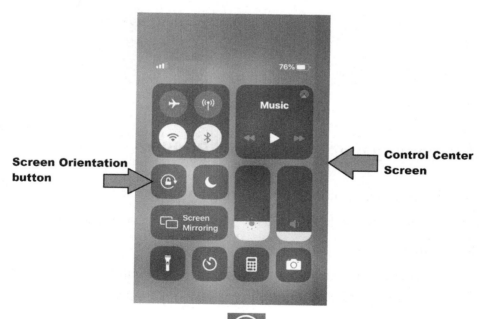

The Portrait orientation lock icon [icon] should appear on the Action Center screen when the screen orientation is locked.

Overcoming the 'Back Button' Problem.

One feature you may quickly find missing if you are used to the
Android platform is a dedicated back button. There is a way to solve
this problem.

- Generally, when you are using an app you should find a
  small back icon (that looks like a triangle) at the top/lower
  left corner of the screen. Tap on this to go back to the
  previous page.

In-App Back Button

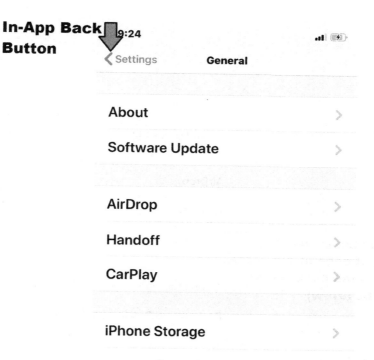

9:24

❮ Settings   **General**

About   >

Software Update   >

AirDrop   >

Handoff   >

CarPlay   >

iPhone Storage   >

- Another way to go back to a previous page is to swipe from the left edge of the screen to the right.

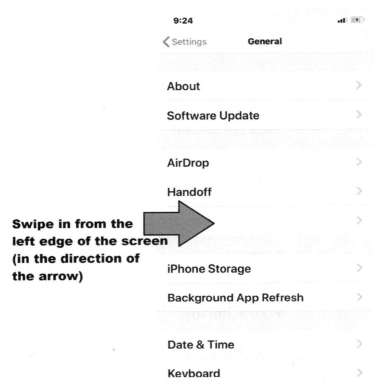

9:24   .ıll ▪️

‹ Settings   **General**

About   ›

Software Update   ›

AirDrop   ›

Handoff   ›

Swipe in from the
left edge of the screen
(in the direction of
the arrow)   ›

iPhone Storage   ›

Background App Refresh   ›

Date & Time   ›

Kevboard   ›

Tip: You may use this option to get out of any applicable page when you are done with the page and you don't see the **done** button.

Getting to Know the Home Screen

From your Home screen, you can view your phone status and access applications. Scroll left or right to see different apps/widgets on the Home screen.

Home Screen Layout

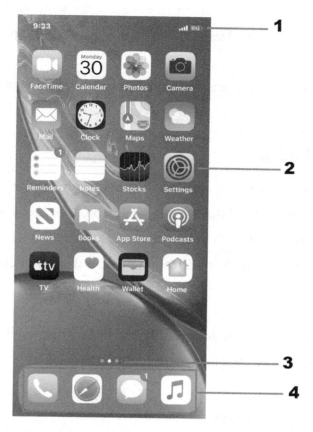

Number	Function
1.	**Status bar**: This is where status icons such as battery icon, Wi-Fi icon, etc. appear.
2.	**App shortcut icon:** Tap any of these icons to launch the corresponding app.
3.	**Home Screen Indicator:** This shows how many Home screens you have, and which one is currently visible.

4.	**iPhone Dock Icons:** These icons are your favorite icons. You can replace these icons with other ones. To learn how to do this, see the next page.

Tip: You can go to the Home Screen by swiping up from the bottom edge of the screen.

Notification badge

If an app has a badge, you can clear this badge by viewing the notification. For example, if the Messaging app has a badge, you can clear this badge by viewing all your new messages.

Please note that a badge is the notification number displayed on an

app icon, e.g. .

Also, you can prevent an app from displaying the notification badge by following the instructions below:

- From the Home screen, tap Settings .
- Tap **Notifications.**
- Scroll down if needed and tap an app. In this case, I have selected the **Messages** app.
- Tap the status switch next to **Badges**.

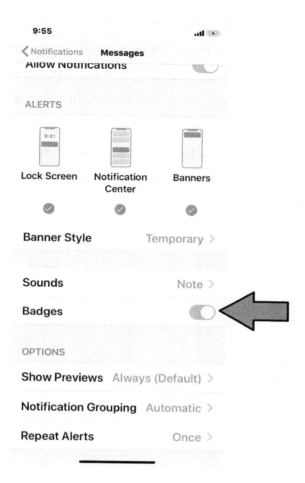

Changing/Rearranging the Dock Icons

The dock icons are the four icons located at the bottom of the Home Screen. You can rearrange or change this icon to the one you like. To do this:

1. Long-press an icon until the icons begin to shake or a small **X** icon appears and then lift your finger. You can long-press any of the dock icons. You may need to press the icon for three to four seconds.

Tip: When you press and hold an app, some options will appear. Don't remove your finger when these options appear. Instead, continue to tap and hold until the apps on the Home screen begin to shake. When this occurs, lift your finger.

2. Thereafter, tap and hold an icon and then drag it to a new location. To add a new icon to the dock icons screen, you may first need to remove an icon to create space for the icon you want to add.

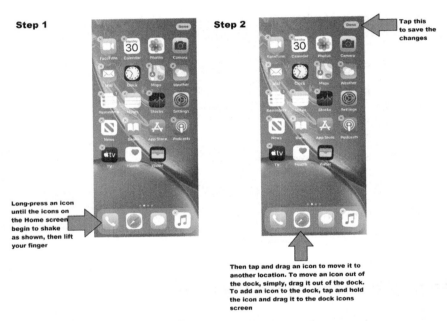

Step 1

Step 2

Tap this to save the changes

Long-press an icon until the icons on the Home screen begin to shake as shown, then lift your finger

Then tap and drag an icon to move it to another location. To move an icon out of the dock, simply, drag it out of the dock. To add an icon to the dock, tap and hold the icon and drag it to the dock icons screen

3. Tap on **Done** found at the top of the screen (see the picture above) to save the changes.

Managing the Home Screen

To get more out of the Home screen, you will need to perform some tweaks.

- To move an app to another location on the Home screen, tap and hold an app until it starts to shake and then lift your finger. Then tap and drag the app to another location on the Home screen. Tap **Done** found at the top of the screen to save your arrangement. To move an app to a different Home screen, drag the app to the edge of the screen and wait for the screen to change.

Note: You might need to press and hold the app for four seconds for the apps to shake. If you press and hold for one second, you will get **Haptic Touch** (see page 172) options instead.

- To remove an app from *iPhone dock* (the four bottom icons), tap and hold the icon until it begins to shake and then lift your finger. Then tap and drag it out of the dock and drop it at the main Home screen. Tap the **Done** button found at the top of the screen to save your arrangement. You can also drag any app from the main Home screen to the *iPhone dock* to replace the removed app.

Tip:

- If you make a mistake and you wish to return your apps to the original arrangement, you can do so by following these steps. Go to **Settings** > **General** > **Reset**, then tap

Reset Home Screen Layout to return the Home screen and apps to their original layout.

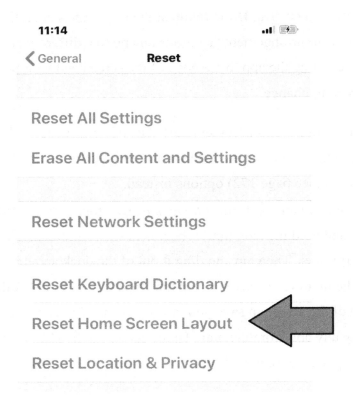

Home Screen Widgets

- To view widgets, swipe right from the left edge of the screen while on the Home screen.

 **Widget screen**

To add more widgets, tap **Edit** (see the screenshot below) and then tap the plus icon next to the widget you want to add. To remove a widget, tap the minus icon next to the widget you want to remove and then tap **Remove**. Tap **Done** found at the top of the screen to save changes.

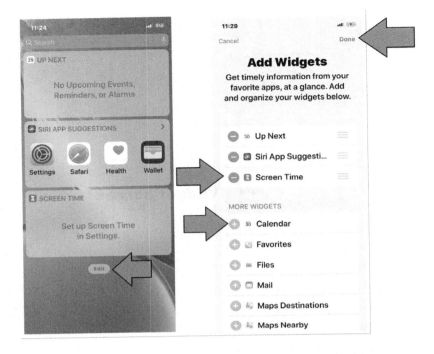

Managing the Home Screen Wallpaper

You can change the wallpaper settings for the Home screen and the locked screen.

1. While on the Home screen, tap on **Settings** . To go to the Home screen from any screen, swipe up from the bottom edge of the screen.)

2. Tap on **Wallpaper**.

3. Tap **Choose a New Wallpaper**.

4. Tap **Stills, Live** or **Dynamic**.

5. Tap the desired photo or wallpaper.

6. Tap **Set** (located in the lower-right).

7. Tap an option:

a. Set Lock Screen

b. Set Home Screen

c. Set Both

Creating a folder of items/apps

1. From the Home screen, tap and hold an app until it starts to shake and then lift your finger. Then tap, drag and drop it onto another item/app to create a folder. Tap the **Done** button found at the top of the screen when you finish. *Please note that you may need to tap and hold for four seconds before the apps begin to shake.*

2. To rename a folder, tap the folder, and then tap and hold an app inside the folder until the apps begin to shake. Thereafter, tap the **X** icon next to the name you want to change and enter a new name. Tap **Done** on the virtual keyboard after entering a name.

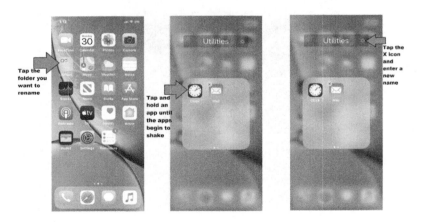

3. To add another app, from the Home screen, tap and hold an app you want to add until it begins to shake. When this occurs, lift your finger. Thereafter, tap, drag and drop the app onto a folder. Tap **Done** found at the top of the screen to save the changes.

4. To delete a folder, remove all the apps inside the folder. To remove an app from a folder, tap the folder. Then tap and hold an app inside the folder until the apps begin to shake. When this happens, lift your finger. Thereafter, tap, hold and drag the app you want to remove out of the folder.

The folder will be deleted automatically after you remove all the apps inside it.

Accessing Applications

1. From the Home screen, tap on the app of your choice.

2. To go back to the app grid screen, swipe up from the bottom edge of the screen.

Accessing Recently Opened or Running Applications

1. To access opened apps, swipe up from the bottom of the screen, and pause. Then lift your finger. A list of recently used apps appears on the screen.

Swipe up and hold for one second to access the app switcher screen

2. A preview window for each app will be displayed. Swipe the apps from left to right to view more apps.

3. To launch an app, tap on it.

4. To close an app, swipe up its preview window.

Uninstall an App

1. While on the Home screen, tap and hold the app you want to uninstall until it begins to shake. You may need to tap and hold for up to four seconds before the apps begin to shake.

2. Tap the **X** next to the app you want to uninstall.

3. Tap **Delete** when prompted.

4. Tap **Done** found at the top of the screen to save the changes.

Understanding the Control Center

The Control Center provides quick access to device functions such as Wi-Fi, allowing you to turn them on and off quickly.

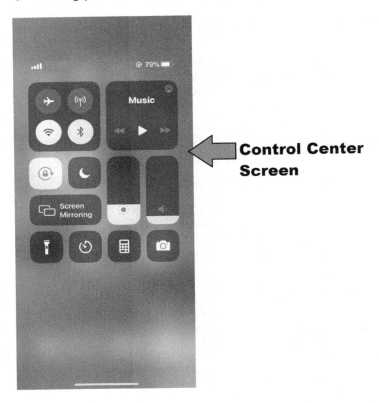

Control Center Screen

To view Control Center:

1. Swipe down from the top-right edge of the screen. You can also do this while on the lock screen.
2. Tap an icon to turn a feature on or off.
3. To access more network options, tap and hold the network card.

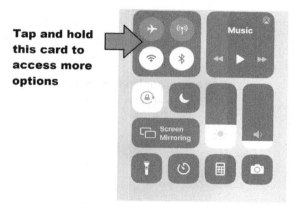

Tap and hold this card to access more options

4. Swipe up from the bottom of the screen to dismiss the Control Center.

Tip: If there is a function/option that you will like to easily and quickly access, you can add it to the Control Center. To add an option to the Control Center, go to **Settings** > **Control Center** > **Customize Controls**. Then tap the plus icon (+) next to the function/option you want to add. To remove an option, tap the red minus icon next to the option you want to remove.

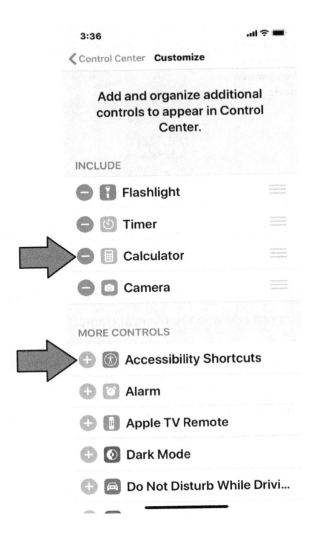

Managing Phone Notifications

Notifications consume battery power, and it may be a source of
disturbance occasionally. To manage notifications:

1. From the Home screen, tap .

2. Then tap **Notifications**.

3. To manage when your iPhone shows notification preview, tap **Show Previews** and choose an option.

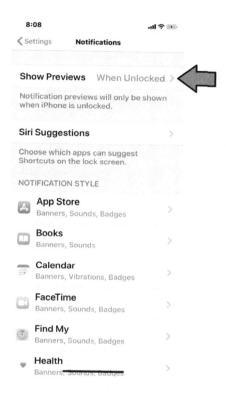

4. Tap an app from the list. In this example, *Book* is selected.

5. If you don't want a notification sound from the chosen app, tap the status switch next to **Sounds**. If you don't want a notification banner form the app, unselect the check circle next to **Banners**. To manage the app notification preview, tap **Show Previews** and choose an option.

Hint: To quickly view your notifications, swipe down from the top-left edge of the screen. Then swipe right to open the notification or swipe left to manage, view or clear the notification.

Tip: To quickly activate/deactivate silent mode on your iPhone, move the silent mode button (see the arrow below) up or down.

Customizing Your Phone

You can get more things done with your phone by customizing it to match your preferences.

Changing your language

1. From the Home screen, tap **Settings** 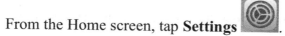.
2. Tap **General**.
3. Scroll down and tap **Language & Region**.

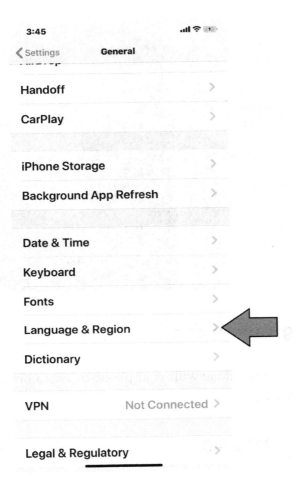

Settings **General**

Handoff >

CarPlay >

iPhone Storage >

Background App Refresh >

Date & Time >

Keyboard >

Fonts >

Language & Region >

Dictionary >

VPN   Not Connected >

Legal & Regulatory >

4. Tap **iPhone Language** and then select a language from the
list.

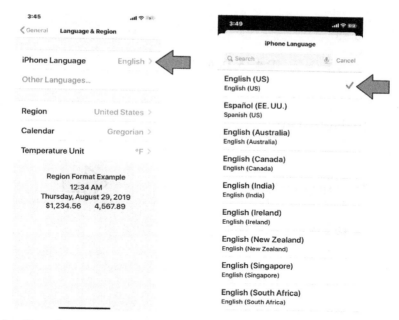

5. Tap **Change...** when prompted.

Setting the current time and date

Your device is built to update its time automatically, but you may need to manually set your time for one reason or the other. To manually set time and date:

1. From the Home screen, tap **Settings** .
2. Tap **General**.
3. Scroll down and tap **Date & Time.**
4. To ensure that the time on your device is updated automatically, enable the switch next to **Set Automatically**.

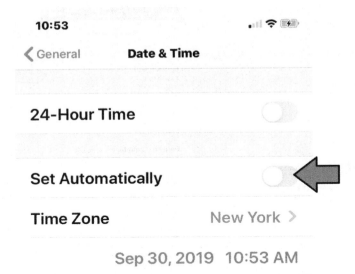

5. To set the time on your device manually or prevent your device from updating the time automatically, disable the switch next to **Set Automatically**, and then edit the time and date as you desire. Please note that you may not be able to set your time manually if Screen Time is enabled. Go to page 175 to learn more about Screen Time.

6. To manage the time zone settings, disable the switch next to **Set Automatically**, and then tap **Time Zone** and choose a time zone.

7. To use a 24-hour time setting for your device, disable the switch next to **24-Hour Time**.

❮ General   **Date & Time**

24-Hour Time ⬤

Set Automatically ⬤

Time Zone New York **❯**

Sep 30, 2019   10:55

Controlling sounds and vibrations

1. From the Home screen, tap **Settings** .
2. Scroll down and tap **Sounds & Haptics**.
3. Tap an option.

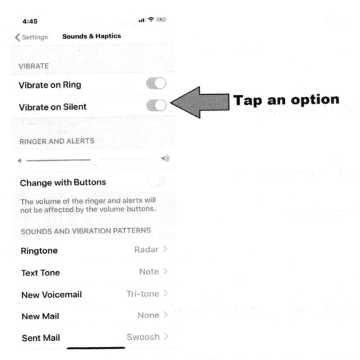

4. To control the volume of ringer and alerts, drag the small circle on the volume slider.

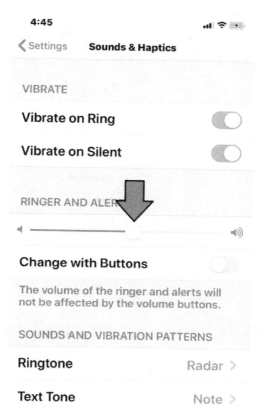

< Settings   **Sounds & Haptics**

VIBRATE

Vibrate on Ring

Vibrate on Silent

RINGER AND ALER

Change with Buttons

The volume of the ringer and alerts will
not be affected by the volume buttons.

SOUNDS AND VIBRATION PATTERNS

Ringtone   Radar >

Text Tone   Note >

5. If you don't want an alert to give a sound, for example, if you
   don't want to receive sound when you get calendar alerts, tap
   Calendar Alerts and then tap **None.**

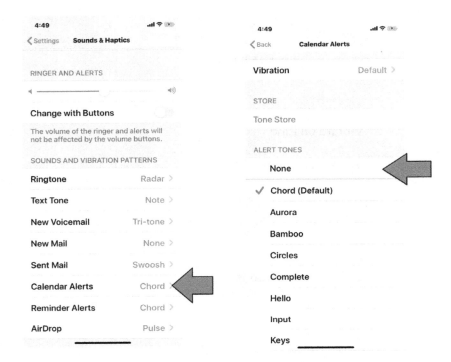

Adjusting the phone volume

Press the Volume up or down key, these keys are located at the left side of your phone (when the phone is facing you).

Setting Home and lock screen image

You can set a Home screen, lock screen or Home and lock screen image to the one of your choice. To do this, please refer to the page 28 above.

Adjusting the brightness of the display

1. Swipe down from the top-right edge of the screen. Then drag the slider as you like to adjust the brightness.

Hint: The brightness level of the display will affect how quickly your device consumes battery power. I will recommend that you turn it reasonably low if you are very concerned about saving battery power.

Also, when auto-brightness/True Tone is turned on, the brightness will adjust automatically depending on the ambient lighting conditions. To disable this feature, go to **Settings** > **Display & Brightness.** Then tap the switch next to **True Tone**.

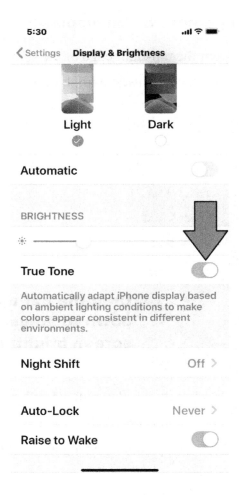

Adjusting the Font Size on Your Phone

You can change the font on your phone to a bigger or smaller font by following the steps below:

1. From the Home screen, tap **Settings** .
2. Tap **Display & Brightness**.

3. Select **Text Size** and adjust the slider as you want. You would see the preview of font size at the upper part of the screen.

Adjust this slider as you want

4. To make the font appear boldened, tap **Bold Text**. Boldening the text makes it easier to see.

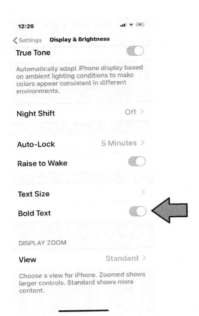

Tip: If you have a senior that has a problem seeing what is on the screen, you could increase the font/text size using the method above. In addition, you can even get a bigger text by going to **Settings**

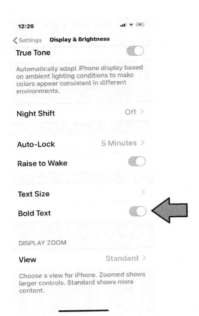 > **Accessibility** > **Display & Text Size** > **Larger Text**. Then tap the status switch next to **Larger Accessibility Sizes** and then use the slider to control the text size.

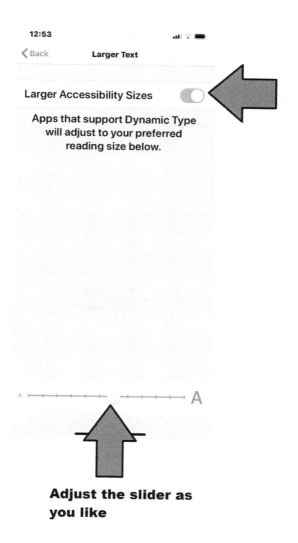

**Adjust the slider as
you like**

Activating the lock screen

You can lock your phone by activating the lock screen feature.

Note: Once you set a screen lock, your phone may require an unlock code each time you turn it on or unlock the touch screen.

1. From the Home screen, tap **Settings** .

2. Scroll down and tap **Face ID & Passcode**.

3. Tap **Turn Passcode On**.

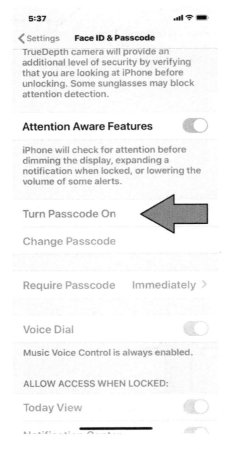

4. Enter a 6-digit passcode. Re-enter your passcode.

5. To turn off passcode, tap **Turn Passcode Off**.

6. To customize what you can do while the screen is locked scroll down to **Allow Access When Locked**, and tap switch next to an item you want to disable or enable.

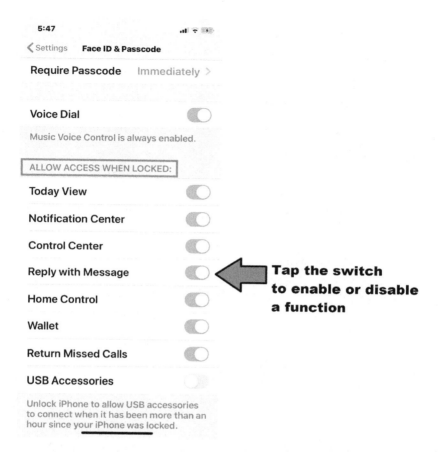

〈 Settings   **Face ID & Passcode**

Require Passcode   Immediately 〉

Voice Dial

Music Voice Control is always enabled.

ALLOW ACCESS WHEN LOCKED:

Today View

Notification Center

Control Center

Reply with Message   ⬅ **Tap the switch**
to enable or disable
Home Control   **a function**

Wallet

Return Missed Calls

USB Accessories

Unlock iPhone to allow USB accessories to connect when it has been more than an hour since your iPhone was locked.

7. If you want your phone to erase all the data on it after 10 failed passcode attempts, tap the status switch next to **Erase Data**. Tap **Enable** if prompted.

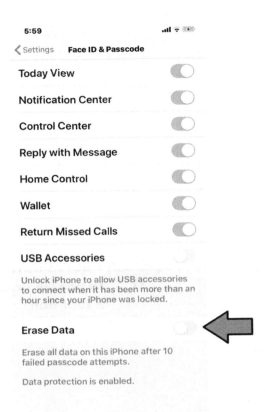

To learn how to unlock your iPhone using your face, see page 62.

Tip: You can tell your device to wake up whenever you pick it up from a surface. To do this, from the Home screen, tap **Settings** > **Display & Brightness** > **Raise to Wake** and tap the status switch to activate this option. Please note that this option may consume your battery faster when enabled.

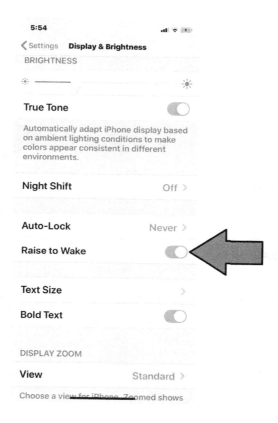

Changing Your iPhone Name

The name of your iPhone is used by iTunes and iCloud.

To change the name of your iPhone:

1. From the Home screen, tap **Settings** .
2. Tap **General**.
3. Tap **About**.
4. Tap **Name** and enter a new name.

Name	Pharm's iPhone >
Software Version	13.1.1

Entering a Text

You can enter a text by selecting characters on the virtual keypad or by speaking words into the microphone through the use of voice command.

Note: You can change the writing language to anyone supported. For more information, please see page 58-59.

To enter a text:

1. Enter a text by selecting the corresponding alphabets or numbers.
2. You can use any of the following keys:

Please note that the on-screen keyboard on your phone may be different from the one shown below. This is because the on-screen keyboard you see depends on the text input field you selected or the network of the phone. The one shown below is the one you should see when you want to compose a text message.

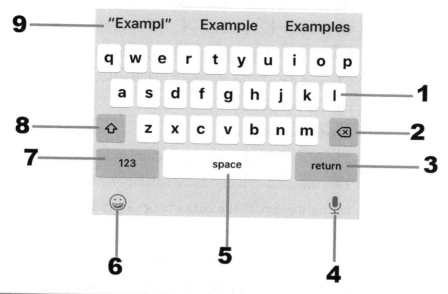

Number	Function
1.	**Virtual Alphabet**. To type an alternate character, tap and hold an alphabet and then slide your finger to choose an option.
2.	**Clear your input/backspace**.
3.	**Start a new line**. It also acts as **Go/Done** button.
4.	**Voice input**. Tap this to type with your voice.
5.	**Space bar**: Use this button to insert space between words. To quickly put a full stop and space after a word, simply double-tap the space bar. To enable this feature, go to **Settings > General > Keyboard > Shortcut**.
6.	**Emoticons button**. To go back to ABC functions after pressing the emoticons key, tap **ABC**. *When you press and hold this key, you will access more*

	functions like Keyboard settings and One-Handed keyboard.
7.	Switch between ABC and Number/Symbol mode.
8.	**Change case**. To permanent upper case, double-tap this button.
9.	**Predictive text bar** **Tip**: Your phone has an auto-correction feature. This means that it can automatically replace a wrong word with the correct one. To enable or disable auto-correction, go to **Settings** > **General** > **Keyboard** > **Auto-Correction**. Besides, the keyboard will show texts suggestion as you type. To use a suggestion, simply tap it.

Hints:

Your keyboard suggests words as you type. You can tap on any suggestion to choose it.

Adding keyboard input languages

1. From the Home screen, tap **Settings** .
2. Tap **General**.
3. Tap **Keyboard**.
4. Tap **Keyboards** to view a list of saved keyboards.
5. Tap **Add New Keyboard...** Tap the keyboard you wish to add. If needed, tap **Done** found at the top of the screen

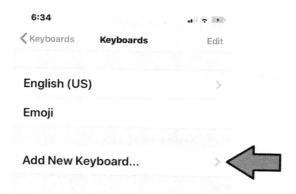

When you select two or more languages, you can switch between the

input languages by tapping on 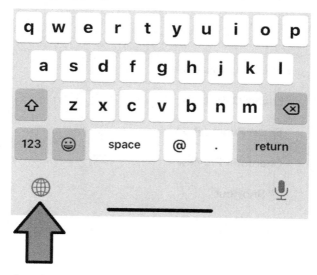.

Please note that the icon shown above may not appear on your keyboard if you have not added more than one language to the keyboard.

Tip: You can customize your virtual keyboard the way you like. To do this:

1. From the Home screen, tap **Settings** .

2. Tap **General**.

3. Tap **Keyboard** and tap an option.

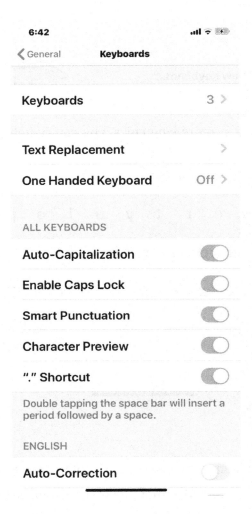

Copying and pasting text(s)

While you are entering a text, you can use the copy and paste feature to copy and paste text(s) from one application to another.

To do this:

1. Double-tap or tap and hold a word, and then drag ┃ or ● to select the texts you want.

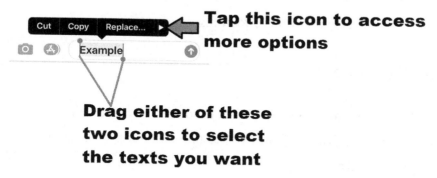

Tap this icon to access more options

Drag either of these two icons to select the texts you want

2. Select the **Copy** option to copy, or select the **Cut** option to cut the text(s) onto the clipboard.

3. In another application or where you want to place the text, tap and hold or double-tap the text input field.

4. Select the **Paste** option to insert the text from the clipboard into the text input field.

Using The Special Features

iPhone 11, iPhone 11 Pro and iPhone 11 Pro Max come with special features that differentiate them from other smartphones. I will now explain how to use some of these features.

Using the Face ID

One of the cool features on iPhone 11, iPhone 11 Pro and iPhone 11 Pro Max is the Face ID. It allows you to unlock your phone without entering passwords.

Registering Your Face ID

1. From the Home screen, tap **Settings** .
2. Tap **Face ID & Passcode**.
3. If you have set up a passcode, you will need to enter it. If you have not, you may need to set up one.
4. Tap **Set Up Face ID**.

USE FACE ID FOR:

iPhone Unlock

iTunes & App Store

Apple Pay

Password AutoFill

iPhone can recognize the unique, three-
dimensional features of your face to allow
secure access to apps and payments.
About Face ID & Privacy...

Set Up Face ID

ATTENTION

Require Attention for Face ID

TrueDepth camera will provide an
additional level of security by verifying
that you are looking at iPhone before
unlocking. Some sunglasses may block

5. Read the onscreen instruction and tap **Get Started**.

6. Carefully follow the onscreen instructions to set up the Face ID.

7. Tap on **Continue**.

8. Follow the onscreen again to register your Face.

9. Tap **Done** when you are through with the setup.

10. If you have not done so before, you may need to enter a backup passcode.

11. If you would like to use the Face ID to unlock your phone, make sure the status switch next to **iPhone Unlock** is enabled.

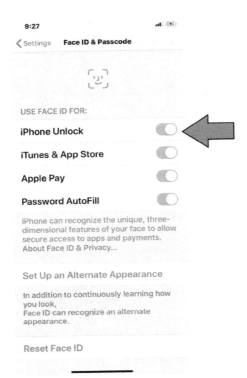

12. In addition, if you would like to use the Face ID with Apple Pay, iTunes & App Store and Password Autofill, make sure the status switch next to each one of them is enabled.

13. To unlock your phone when your phone locks, press the side key and look at the phone. Then swipe to open.

Deleting your Face ID

1. From the Home screen, tap **Settings** .

2. Tap **Face ID & Passcode**.

3. If you have set up a passcode, you will need to enter it.

4. Tap **Reset Face ID**.

Water Resistance

Another feature that makes iPhone 11, iPhone 11 Pro, and iPhone 11 Pro Max unique is the water resistance. You don't have to worry that your phone is going to get wet when you are inside the rain. To know more about water resistance, please go to page 12-13.

Siri

Siri is a trained virtual assistant that has been built to answer questions, and interestingly, you probably don't need any technical training to use this feature. If you need any, it will be some tweaks and how to ask questions. That is what this section of the guide is mainly for. This section of the guide will show you how to manage Siri like a maven and how to ask questions and give commands that Siri will understand.

Getting Started with Siri

You should have the option to set up Siri when you first start using your phone. If you skip this step during the phone setup and you will like to do it now, then go to the phone settings 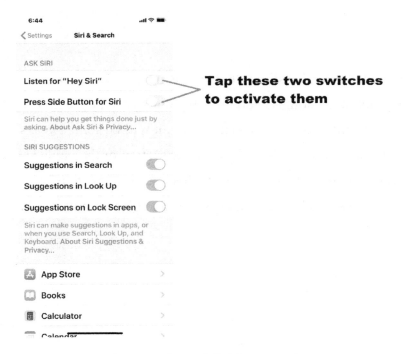 and select **Siri & Search**. Then tap the switches next to **Listen for "Hey Siri"** and **Press Side Button for Siri**. If prompted to enable Siri, select **Enable Siri** and carefully follow the onscreen instructions to finish the setup.

1. You can get the attention of Siri in several ways:

   • Press the side button until Siri function appears. Then make a command.

- Say **Hey Siri** and then make your request. Please note that you may need to enable this feature. To do this, **Settings** > **Siri & Search**. Then tap the switch next to **Listen for "Hey Siri"**.

2. An audio wave moves across your screen, letting you know Siri is listening and processing your request.

3. To give another command to Siri, tap the **continue to listen** button (located at the bottom of the screen) or say **Hey Siri** followed by the command.

4. To get example commands, tap the question mark icon found at the bottom of the screen.

Note: You may notice that the question you asked Siri is different from what it types on the screen (what Siri types on the screen is what it thought you have said), I will advise that you always try to speak clearly.

Understanding Siri's Interface

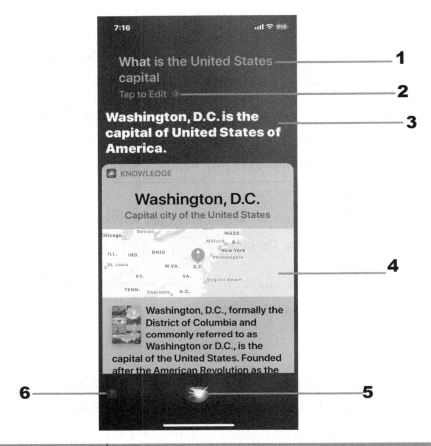

Number	Function
1.	Your Question
2	Tap this to edit a command using the onscreen keyboard.
3.	Siri's Response
4.	More info tab. You can scroll down this tab to access more information or access website links.
5.	Tap this icon to continue speaking to Siri.

| 6. | Tap on this to access the help page. |

Getting What You Want from Siri

There are many things you can ask Siri to do for you and before you finish reading this guide you will learn how to effectively interact with it.

I will like to mention that interacting with Siri is not an examination (so there is nothing like cheating) and you can get help by tapping on the question mark icon on the Siri menu. You can also ask Siri **"What can you do?"**.

Allowing Siri to Access Your Apps

You can choose how apps behave with Siri:

1. From the Home screen, tap **Settings** .
2. Tap **Siri & Search**.
3. Scroll down, tap an app, and then tap the status switch next to **Show Siri Suggestions** or **Show in Search**. You may also deactivate other options if you like.

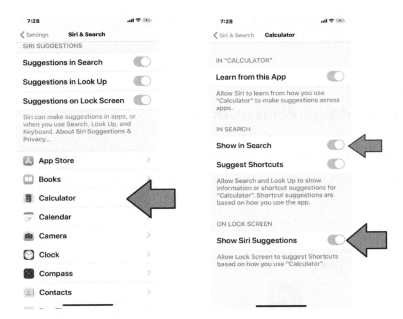

Using Siri to Open Apps or Programs

One of those things you may want Siri to do is opening your apps. You can quickly open an app by saying **Open** and then mentioning the name of the app. For example, to open Settings, say **Open settings.** To open calculator, say **Open calculator**.

You may also say **Launch settings** instead of **Open settings.**

In addition, you may give a more specific command like **Open sound settings** to go to sound settings. Say **Launch Wi-Fi Settings** to open the Wi-Fi settings.

Using Siri with Calendar

One of the fantastic features that Siri can do for you is making an appointment. This virtual assistant is fully integrated with your device Calendar making it easy for it to make appointments for you.

With just a few commands, you can get Siri to put an event or appointment into your calendar. To do this:

1. Press the side button until Siri function appears.

2. Alternatively, you can get Siri's attention by saying **Hey Siri**.

3. Then say whatever you want to include in the Calendar. For example, you can say the following:

    - Create an appointment with Clinton for Monday at 1 p.m.

    - Schedule a conference with John at 10 a.m. on Sunday.

    - Meet with Ibrahim at noon. Please note that you can also say all the examples given above in other ways. The most important thing is to get Siri to understand what you are saying.

    - When it has gotten the information, the Calendar will appear on the Siri menu. You can then say **Confirm/Yes** if you are satisfied with the response. If not, say **Cancel.**

You can also make changes to your Calendar using Siri. To do this:

1. Repeat the first step above.

2. Then say what you want it to change. For example, you may say any of the following:

   - Change the appointment scheduled with Clinton on Monday at 1 p.m. to 3 p.m.

   - Cancel my schedule with John.

   - Cancel my appointment scheduled for 10 a.m. on Sunday.

In addition, you can check how your Calendar looks like today. To do this

Tap the **continue to listen** icon and say, "**How does my calendar look like today?**" Or say, "**Do I have any appointment today**?" Or just any variant. Note that you can also ask Siri about your Calendar for a day in the future. To do this, say "**Do I have any appointment scheduled for tomorrow**".

Using Siri to Setup Reminders

There are probably many things going through your mind and it will be quite interesting if you can get a personal assistant to assist in remembering some of your duties. Interestingly, Siri can help you in this regard.

To set a reminder using Siri:

1. Press the side button until Siri function appears.

2. Alternatively, you can get Siri's attention by saying **Hey Siri**.

3. Then say whatever you want to include in the Reminder. For example, you can say the following:

   - Remind me to fix the car by 3 p.m.

   - Remind me to drop the cake at the restaurant.

   - Remind me to pick my daughter by 4 p.m.

   - Remind me to call Ibrahim at 1 p.m.

4. When it has gotten the information, the reminder will appear. You can change the reminder by tapping on **Change**.

Please note that it is not compulsory that you put remind in every statement as I did above, but I will advise that you do this whenever you can. This is because it will help Siri to easily get what you are saying and avoid any confusion.

Using Siri with Alarm

You can also set an alarm using this personal assistant. To do this:

1. Press the side button until Siri function appears.

2. Alternatively, you can get Siri's attention by saying **Hey Siri**.

3. Say the time for alarm. For example, you can say: "**set an alarm for 1 p.m. tomorrow**" or "**alarm for 1 p. m tomorrow**". Please note that Siri may be unable to set an alarm for more than one day (around 24 hours) ahead.

4. You may also say **set an everyday alarm for 3 P.M.**

5. When it has gotten the information, the alarm will appear, and it will tell you that it has set the alarm.

Using Siri with Clock

You can ask Siri what your local time is. In addition, it can also tell you the time in a specific place.

1. Press the side button until Siri function appears.

2. Alternatively, you can get Siri's attention by saying **Hey Siri**.

3. Then say, "**What is the time?**" or say, "**What is the time in New York?**"

Using Siri to Get Flight Information

You can also use this virtual assistant to get information about a flight. This is a smarter way to know when an airplane will take off.

For example, you can say "**What is the flight status of Delta 400?**" to get the flight information about this flight.

You may also say **How much does it cost to travel from Florida to Washington by plane**.

Using Siri with Weather App

To know about the weather, just say **"What's the weather going to be today?"**. You may also know about the weather condition of a place by asking **"What is the weather of New York today?"**.

Using Siri with Mail App/ Message App

You can instruct Siri to compose an email/message for you. To do this:

1. Press the side button until Siri function appears.

2. Alternatively, you can get Siri's attention by saying **Hey Siri**.

3. Then say the subject and the person you want to email. For example, you can say:

   - Send an email to Ibrahim about the meeting.

   - Email Ibrahim and say I got the message, thanks.

   - Send an SMS to Clinton

   - Any new email from Ibrahim today?

   - Show the email from John yesterday.

- Reply John, sorry about not coming for the meeting.

Please note that you may need to enable some apps before Siri can communicate with them. Please refer to page 69-70 to in the subsection above to learn more.

In addition, note that you will usually have to include one or more information before you can send the email. For example, you will need to say the body of the email before you send it.

Using Siri with Map App

You can also use Siri to search the map. This virtual assistant is fully integrated with the Map app on your device. To get how the map of a place looks like:

1. Say **Hey Siri**.

2. Then say the map of an area you want to get. For example, you may say:

   - Show me the New York map.

   - Show me the map of Seattle.

   - Give me the directions to John F. Kennedy International Airport.

What about Math?

Siri can also help you with some mathematics and conversions. For example, you can tell Siri **"What is the square root of four?"**. You may also say **"convert one foot to centimeter"** or **"Convert dollars to pounds?"** or **"what is 100 factorial"** and so on. As I have said before, the most important thing is to make sure Siri gets the message you are trying to get across.

Using Siri to Get Meanings of Words

You can quickly check for the meaning of a word by asking Siri. For example, you may say **"What is the meaning of flabbergasted?"**.

Siri's Settings/Options

The tab under Siri allows you to manage Siri's functions. To access these options:

1. From the Home screen, tap **Settings** .
2. Tap **Siri & Search**.

The options may include:

Listen for "Hey Siri": If this option is enabled, you will be able to get the attention of Siri by saying **Hey Siri**.

Allow Siri When Locked: This option allows you to access Siri from the lock screen.

Language: Allows you to change the language of Siri.

Siri Voice: Use this option to select Siri Voice.

Voice Feedback: Tap this option to customize feedback settings.

My Information: Tap this for your information.

Troubleshooting Siri

Although much effort has been put into making this virtual assistant, I am quite sure that Siri will misbehave at one time or the other. When this happens, there are few things to do.

- **Ensure that you are connected to a strong network**: If you have a bad or no internet connection, Siri may not work properly. Therefore, the first thing to check when Siri starts to misbehave is the internet connection.

- **Speak clearly in a silent place**: Make sure you are speaking clearly and try to avoid background noise.

- **Tap the continue listen button**: Tap (found at the bottom of the screen) if the device does not hear you, or to give it another command.

- **Try to restart your smartphone**: If you find out that all that I have mentioned above does not work, you may try restarting your device.

Using the Web

Safari App

Opening the Safari

1. From the Home screen, tap **Safari** icon.

Get to Know the Safari's Interface

The image below will introduce you to various buttons found on Safari:

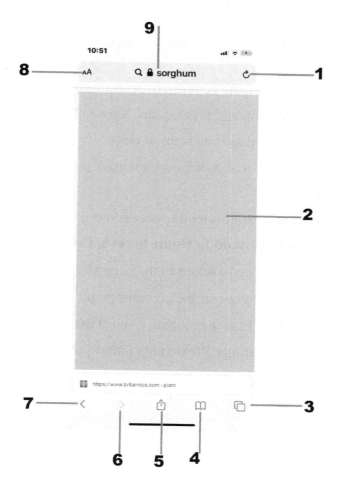

1	**Refresh: Tapping this icon reloads a webpage.**
2	**Webpage view**: Webpage information is shown here. To zoom, place your two fingers on the screen and spread them apart or do the reverse.
3	**Tabs:** Tap this to navigate between different webpages. To close an app, tap the tab icon and then tap the **X** icon next to the thumbnail of the webpage you want to close.
4	**Bookmark:** Tap this icon to access bookmark pages, reading list, and history.
5	**Menu/Share icon:** Tap this icon to access more options such as **Share, Find on Page, Add to Home Screen, Print**, etc.
6	**Forward**: Tap this icon to return to the page you just left.
7	**Back:** Tap this icon to revisit the previous page.
8	**AA** icon: Tap this to hide the toolbar, request the desktop side or access the website settings. Please note that if you hide the toolbar, you can bring it back into view by double-tapping the URL address found at the top of the screen.
9	**Address bar**: Tapping this bar allows you to enter the web address of a webpage. You may also type in a search phrase into the address bar.

Using the Address/Search Bar

Every web browser must have an address bar and Safari also has one. This bar serves the function of a URL address bar and search bar. You can change the default search engine used by Safari. To learn how to change the search engine to another one, please go to page 90.

You choose whether to launch a webpage or search for a term based on what you type into the address bar. For example, if you type **Infovore Secrets** into the address bar and tap **Go**, Google/Bing search results for that phrase are displayed. On the other hand, if you type **infovoresecrets.com** and tap **Go**, you will be taken to the website bearing the name.

When you begin to type inside the address bar, Safari automatically makes suggestions beneath your typing. You can choose one of these suggestions to make things faster.

If you don't want to see suggested search terms, go to **Settings** > **Safari**. Then turn off **Search Engine Suggestions** and **Safari Suggestions**.

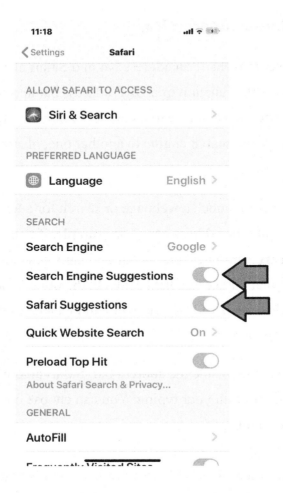

Zooming a Webpage in Safari

To zoom in a webpage in Safari, place two fingers on the webpage and spread them apart. To zoom out, place two fingers on the webpage and move them closer together.

Using Tabs on Safari

The tab's icon allows you to open multiple webpages at once. You can open many tabs at once on Safari. Please see the image under **Get to know Safari's Interface** to have a pictorial view of the Safari tab icon.

To manage the browsing tabs:

1. Tap the tab icon  found at the bottom of the screen. If the tab icon is not showing up scroll up the screen.
2. To open a new tab, tap the + icon.

3. To open a tab, tap the desired tab.

4. To close a tab, tap the **X** icon at the top left corner of the thumbnail of the tab you want to close. See the picture above.

Tip: You can quickly close all the opened webpages by tapping and

holding the tab icon 🗖 . Then tap **Close All ... Tabs**. To close only the current tab, select **Close This Tab**.

Favorites/Bookmarks

With several billions of webpages in the internet world, you just have to select your favorites. Just like other modern-day browsers, Safari gives you the opportunity to select a favorite or bookmark a page. This makes it easier to visit the website or webpage in the future.

To bookmark a webpage:

1. Open the website you want to bookmark.

2. Tap **Menu/Share icon** 📤 (located at the bottom of the screen). You may see the image under **Get to know the Safari's Interface** to have a pictorial view of the menu/share icon.

3. Tap **Add Bookmark** or **Add to Favorites**.

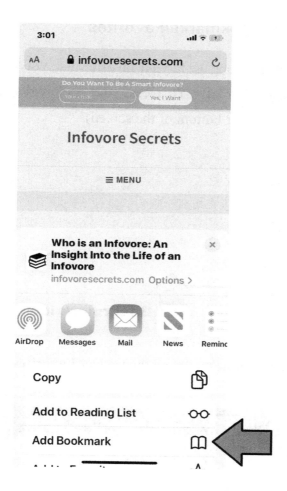

4. Key in the appropriate name for the bookmark or favorite.

5. Tap **Save** found at the top of the screen.

Hint: You can quickly add a webpage to your bookmark list by

tapping and holding the bookmark icon 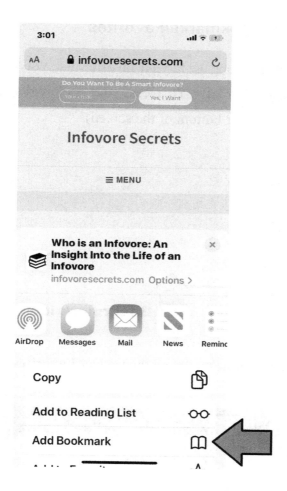. Then select **Add**
Bookmark. You can also select **Add Bookmarks for ... Tabs** to
add all the opened tabs to the bookmark list.

Accessing Your Bookmarks/Favorites

After you have added a webpage to your favorites list, you will need to access this list sooner or later. To access your bookmarks, tap the Bookmarks (located at the bottom of the screen).

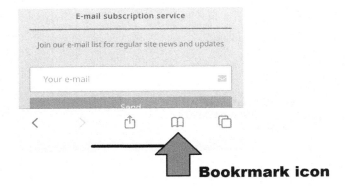

Bookrmark icon

Tap the bookmark tab (if needed) and then select **Favorites**.

Saving a webpage for later reading

Webpages contain a lot of information and you will probably need to schedule some webpages for later reading. Saving a webpage in the reading list is a great way to do this. When you find interesting information online and you don't have the time to read it immediately, you can save it and read it later.

To save a webpage for later reading, open the webpage and tap located at the bottom screen, then tap **Add to Reading List**. If prompted to save articles in your reading list automatically for offline reading, choose **Save Automatically** if needed.

Accessing Your Reading List

After you have saved a page in the reading list, you will need to access this list sooner or later. To do this, tap the Bookmarks (located at the bottom of the screen) and then tap.

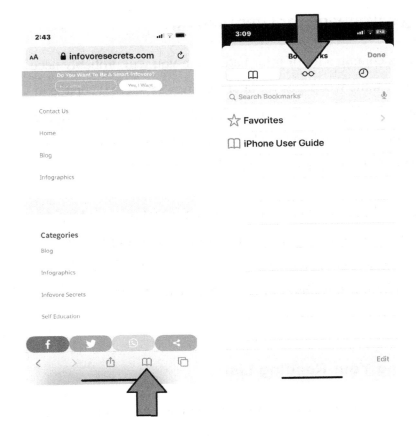

Changing the Search Engine

You may not love the default search engine on Safari, and you may want to change it to another one.

You can change the Safari Search Engine by following the steps highlighted below:

1. From the Home screen, tap **Settings** .
2. Tap **Safari**.

3. Tap on **Search Engine** and select a search engine. Then tap the back button located at the top left corner of the screen.

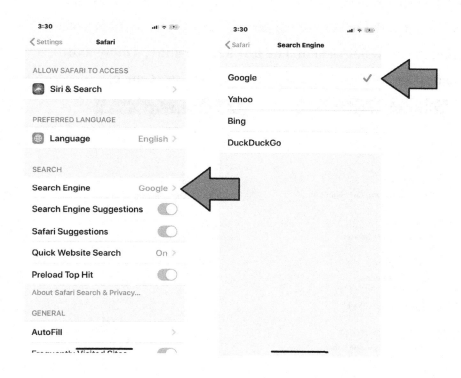

Managing the History List

If the private mode is not enabled, Safari collects the history of the webpages you visit and stores it.

To access your history:

1. Tap the Bookmarks 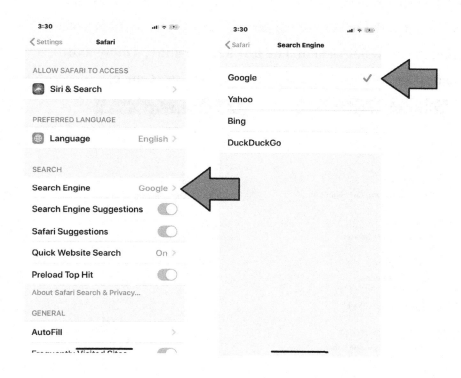 (located at the bottom of the screen).

2. Tap **History** 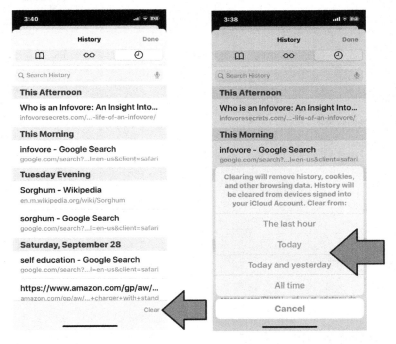.

Hint: To clear browsing data, repeat the two steps above and tap **Clear** found at the bottom of the screen. Then select whether you are clearing the browsing data of **The last hour**; **Today**; **Today and yesterday**; or **All time**. To cancel this process, tap **Cancel**.

To delete a single webpage from the history, simply tap and hold the webpage address and select **Delete**

Tip: If you see that a website/webpage is misbehaving, you can try deleting the history and see if this would solve the problem.

Sharing a Webpage with Friends

To share your webpage with friends, open the Safari app and tap

. Then choose an option from the sharing options that appear.

Private Browsing

There are times when you will not want your browser to save any information about your visit to a webpage. For instance, if you don't want a website to save cookies on your device or you don't want your child to know you are browsing about favorite gifts to buy for them.

In addition, Private mode browsing allows for multiple sessions. For example, you may access your Yahoo mail account (or another web account) on a normal window and use the Private mode tab to open the Yahoo mail account of that of your friend or family member without logging out of your own account. Pages viewed in Private mode are not listed in your browser history or search history and leave no traces (such as cookies) on your device.

To use the Private browsing, tap the tab icon and tap **Private.** Then tap the plus icon (+) to open a webpage in private mode.

To close a webpage in Private mode, tap the tab icon and then tap the **X** next to the thumbnail of the site you want to close.

Please note that you may have to close the webpage opened in private mode to prevent Safari from opening the last webpage you visited in private mode when you open the Safari app again.

To go back to normal browsing, tap the tab button 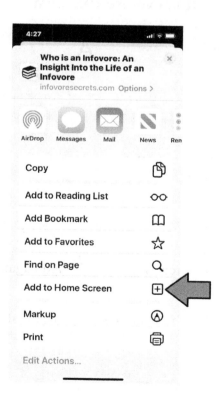 and then tap **Private**.

Add Your Favorite Webpage to the Home Screen

You can make your favorite webpage a shortcut on the Home screen. This allows you to easily access the webpage directly from your Home screen. To do this:

1. Open the webpage and tap on ⬆️.
2. Scroll up and tap **Add to Home Screen**.

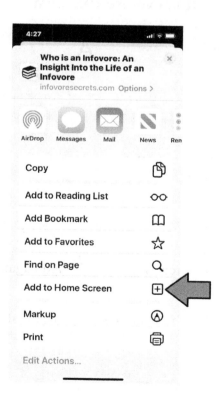

3. Edit the webpage name if needed and select **Add** found at the top of the screen.

Using Distraction-free Reading

Distraction-free reading removes adverts and other distracting items from a webpage. To use this feature, open a webpage and tap on **AA** next to the address bar. Then select **Show Reader View**.

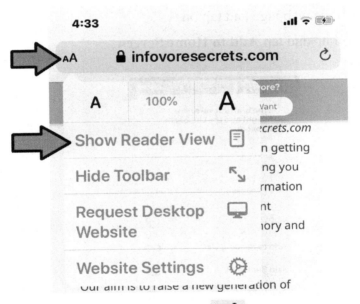

To exit the distraction-free reading, tap **AA** icon again and select **Hide Reader View**.

Please note that this feature may not be available on all webpages.

Revoking the website permissions you have given a website

If you have given a website the permission to use the microphone, location or camera, you can revoke it following the steps below.

1. Open the website you want to manage.

2. Tap on the **AA** icon (found next to the address bar).

3. Select **Website Settings**.

4. Select **Camera**, **Microphone** or **Location** and select an appropriate response.

Tip: If you want a website to open in desktop mode automatically when you open it, repeat steps 1 to 3 above and tap the status switch next to **Request Desktop Website**. You can also use a similar method to open a webpage in Reader's view automatically.

More on the More Options Tab

Many options under the more options tab ⬆️ have already been discussed, but I will still like to point out few more things.

1. **Print:** Use this option to print a webpage. To print a webpage, simply tap **Print** and follow the prompts.

2. **Find on Page:** Use this option to search for a word or a phrase on a webpage.

Tip: To access more options while on the *More Options* screen, swipe up or down.

Using the AA icon

This **AA** icon is found next to the address bar. Tap this icon to access the following:

- **Zoom**: Tap on small **A** to decrease the zoom, or tap on the big **A** to increase the zoom.
- **Show Reader View**: Please refer to page 96 to learn more about this option.
- **Request desktop site:** Use this option to request the desktop version of a webpage.
- **Website Settings**: Tap this to manage the permission you have given a website. For example, if you have given a

website the permission to use the microphone, you can revoke it using this tab.

Troubleshooting Internet Connection when Using Safari

Safari may sometimes refuse to browse the internet. When this happens, you may try any of the suggestions below:

1. Check if you are connected to a Wireless network. If your phone is not connected to a network, from a Home screen, tap **Settings** > **Wi-Fi**. Then tap the status switch to enable the Wi-Fi. When the wireless network is active, you should see this icon on the status bar at the top of the screen.

2. If you are trying to use a cellular connection and not a Wi-Fi connection, then check your cellular data connection. From the Home screen, tap **Settings** > **Cellular** > **Cellular Data**.

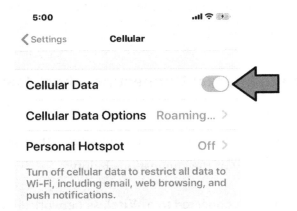

3. If you are trying to roam while abroad, check that you have allowed roaming. From the Home screen, tap **Settings** > **Cellular** > **Cellular Data Options**. Then ensure **Data Roaming** is enabled. Please note that you may need to turn on *Cellular Data* before you can be able to manage Roaming. In addition, please note that when roaming, international roaming charges may apply.

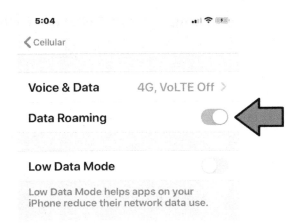

You may contact your network service provider if your phone still refuses to browse after trying all that I have mentioned above.

Communication

Calling

Learn how to use the calling functions, such as making and answering calls, using options available during a call and using call-related features.

Depending on your network service provider, please note that the descriptions in this section of the guide may be different from the one on your device.

When you tap the Phone icon (found on the Home screen), you should see a screen like the one below:

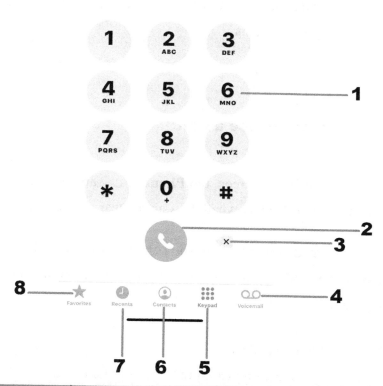

123 456

9 ——————————— Add Number

Number	Function
1.	Keypad numbers.
2.	**Call button**: Tap this to make a call.
3.	**Delete/Backspace**.
4.	**Voicemail button:** Tap this to check your voicemail or set up voicemail.
5.	**Keypad button:** Tap this to show the keypad.

6.	**Contacts**: Tap this to access your contacts.
7.	**Recents**: Tap this to access the call log. To access more information about a call, tap ⓘ.
8.	**Favorites**: Tap this to access your favorite list.
9.	**Add number**: Use this option to add a number to your contacts.

To Make a Call or Silence a Call

1. While on the Home screen, tap **Phone** 📞 and enter a phone number. If the keypad does not appear on the screen, tap the keypad button ⠿ Keypad to show the keypad. To call a number on your contact, tap the **Contact** button on the Phone app screen.

2. Tap 📞 to make a call.

3. To silence an incoming call, press the volume up/down button.

Hint: You can access apps/items on your phone while receiving a call. Swipe up from the bottom edge of the screen to go to the Home Screen and then tap on the item/app you want to access. To return to the call, tap the green bar at the top of the screen.

Green bar

Besides, you can use Siri to call or send a message. To do this, open the Siri app, and say **Call** or **Text** and then the contact's name.

Note: If your phone is not ringing aloud, check if you have not mistakenly enabled the silent mode. To turn on/off the silent mode, flip the ring/silent button located at the side of the phone (the button located next to volume buttons).

To Answer a Call or Reject an Incoming Call:

1. To receive an incoming call, tap **Accept (the green phone icon).**

2. To decline an incoming call, tap **Decline (the red phone icon).**

3. To reply with a text, tap **Message** and then tap one of the pre-written messages or tap **Custom…**, and write your message.

4. To remind yourself to return the call, tap **Remind Me**, then indicate when you want to be reminded.

Note: You can create rejection messages of your own. From the Home screen, tap **Settings** 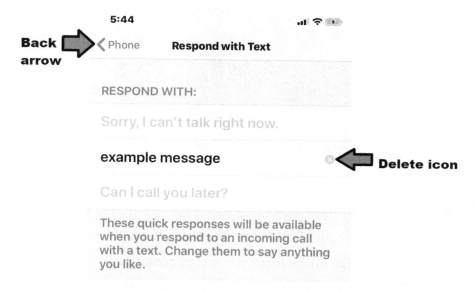 > **Phone** > **Respond with Text**, then tap any of the default messages to edit it. When you are done, tap the back arrow found at the top of the screen. To delete the message you have entered, simply tap the **X** icon (the delete icon) next to the message.

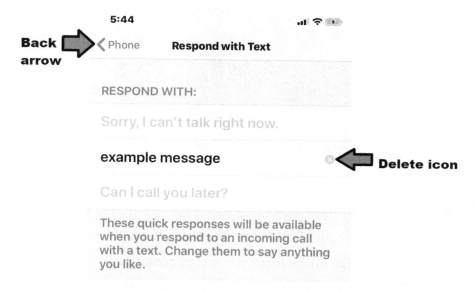

Learn How to Use Your Phone During a Call

You can perform any of these tasks when on a call:

Depending on your network service provider, please note that the image shown below may be different from the one on your device.

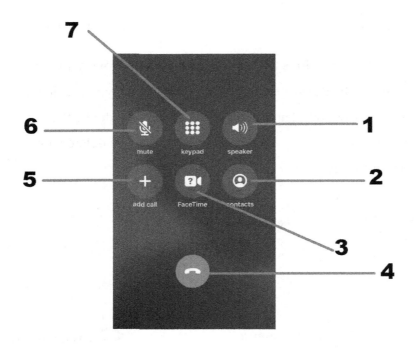

Number	Function
1.	To turn Speakerphone on or off, tap this icon.
2.	Tap contacts to view stored contacts.
3.	Tap FaceTime to initiate a video call with another iOS or Mac OS user.
4.	Tap this icon to end a call.
5.	Tap add call icon to add another number to the call or begin a conference call.
6.	Tap this to mute the microphone.
7.	Tap this icon to access the keypad.

Tip: To access the application screen while on a call, swipe up from the bottom edge of the screen. To return to the call, tap the green bar at the top of the screen.

Green bar

Place a New Call While on a Call (Conference Calling)

If your network service provider supports this feature, you can make another call while a call is in progress.

1. From the active call screen, tap + **Add call**.
2. Choose a contact and tap the call icon.

3. To add a number that isn't in your contacts, tap Keypad Keypad located at the bottom of the screen. Enter the number and

   then tap the Call icon.
4. When the call is answered:

   i.   Tap **Swap** to switch between the two calls.

ii.   Tap **Merge calls** to turn the call to a conference call.

5. To end a call while in the Conference call mode, tap the **info** icon (next to the conference call numbers/contacts) and then tap **End** next to the contact you want to stop talking to.

6. To talk privately with one person in a conference call, tap the Info icon , then tap **Private** next to the person's contact or number. Tap **Merge Calls** to resume the conference call.

7. To end all calls, tap the red key .

Emergency Calling

You can use iPhone 11, iPhone 11 Pro, or iPhone 11 Pro Max to make an emergency call. From the Home screen, tap **Phone** icon and enter the emergency telephone number. Note that if you dial 911 in the U.S, your location details may be provided to the emergency service provider even if your settings do not support this. To make an emergency call from a lock screen, on the Enter Passcode screen, tap **Emergency** and then dial the required number.

Managing Your Recent Tab

When you call a phone number or receive a call from a phone number, they will appear under the recent tab. To access the recent tab:

1. From the Home screen, tap the Phone icon .
2. Select **Recents** found at the bottom of the screen.
3. To only see the missed calls, select **Missed** found at the top of the screen.

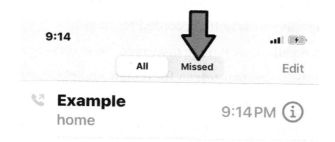

4. To access more details about a contact/number, tap on the icon next to the contact/number.

Voicemail

This option allows you to access your voicemail.

Please note, depending on your service provider, the instructions given below may not be applicable to you.

To set up voicemail:

1. From the Home screen, tap on **phone app** .

2. Tap on **Voicemail** icon Voicemail .

3. If you are using voicemail for the first time, select **Set Up Now**.

4. Enter a 7 to 15-digit voicemail password and select **Done**.

5. Re-enter your voicemail password, and select **Done**.

6. Select a default greeting or record a custom greeting, then select **Done/Save**. If you are selecting **Custom,** tap **Record** to record your personal message and tap **Stop** when you finish. Tap **Save** to save the recorded message.

7. Your Voicemail inbox will be displayed. New messages will appear on the voicemail screen for review and playback. Tap a message to begin playback.

8. To get info about a contact in voicemail, tap the info icon next to the contact.

9. To delete a voicemail message, tap **Delete** while viewing the message.

10. To call back a voicemail contact, tap the phone icon while viewing the message.

Tip: There are some network providers that enable you to set up a voicemail by tapping and holding **1** and following the prompts.

To access and manage your voicemail:

1. From the app grid tap on **phone app** .

2. Tap on **Voicemail** icon Voicemail . You may need to enter a password.

3. Tap on a message you want to listen to.

4. Tap **play icon**.

5. You may also tap on **delete icon** to delete it. When you delete a message, the message may go to Deleted message box. To permanently delete a message, tap **Deleted messages** and tap **Clear All.** Tap **Clear All** again.

Tip: To change a voicemail password, go to **Settings** > **Phone > Change Voicemail Password**.

If the instructions above do not work for you, please contact your network service provider to know how to set up your voicemail.

Using Call Waiting

Call waiting allows you to get another call while you're already on one.

To enable this feature, please go to **Settings** > **Phone > Call waiting**.

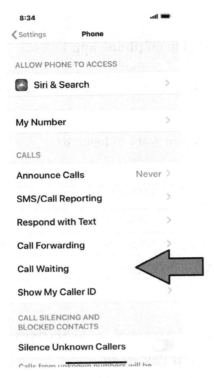

Then make sure the status switch next to **Call Waiting** is switched on.

Depending on your network service provider, please note that the image shown above may be different from the one on your device.

Call Forwarding (Diverting Calls to Another Number)

When you are busy, you can forward incoming calls to another phone number. Please note that your network provider will need to support this feature for it to be available.

To enable this feature:

1. From the Home screen, tap **Settings** .

2. Tap **Phone**.

3. Tap **Call Forwarding**.

4. Tap the status switch next to **Call Forwarding** and enter the number you want to forward your calls to.

5. To disable this feature, repeat steps 1 to 3 above and tap the indicator switch next to **Call Forwarding**.

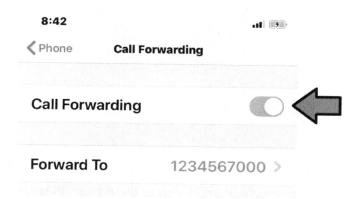

Please note that when the call forwarding option is enabled, you should see the call forwarding icon when you access the Action Center. To access the Action Center, swipe down from the top right egde of the screen.

In addition, depending on your network provider, you may be able to forward calls to your voicemail and listen to them later. Please contact your network service provider to learn how to do this.

Block Calls

If your service provider supports this feature, you may be able to avoid receiving calls from certain numbers.

Please note that call blocking feature may not affect phone calls made or received via apps (e.g. Skype) installed on your device. Also, note that the features available under Call blocking may differ from one service provider to another.

To block a contact:

1. From the Home screen, tap **Settings** .

2. Tap **Phone**.

3. Tap **Block Contacts**

4. Select **Add New...**

5. Tap the contact you would like to block.

6. To unblock a contact, tap **Edit** located at the top of the screen, then tap the minus (-) icon next to the contact and then tap **Unblock.**

Tip: To block calls from an anonymous number or an unknown number, turn on 'Do Not Disturb' manually and set it to allow calls from your contacts list. To learn more about Do Not Disturb, please see page 185.

In addition, you can silence and send calls from unknown numbers (not saved in your phonebook) to voicemail. To do this: go to

Settings ⚙ > Phone > Silence Unknown Callers.

When Silence Unknown Callers is enabled, calls from phone numbers not saved in your phonebook are diverted to your voicemail and it will appear as missed calls under the Recents tab. To access the Recents tab, open the Phone app 📞 and tap on Recents found at the bottom of the screen.

Hint: If a strange number is disturbing you with unnecessary calls, you can block the number if needed. To do this:

1. From the Home screen, tap the Phone icon 📞.

2. Select Recents found at the bottom of the screen and tap on the ⓘ icon next to the number you want to block.

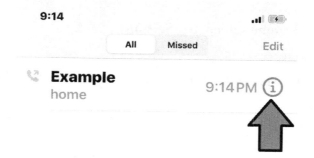

3. Scroll down and select **Block this Caller**. Read the onscreen cautionary note, and choose **Block Contact** if you agree.

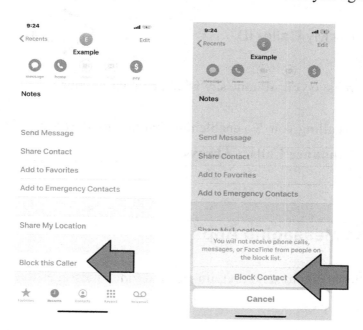

What about Caller ID?

If your service provider supports this feature, you may prevent your service provider from displaying your number(ID) when you call another person.

1. From the Home screen, tap **Settings** .

2. Tap **Phone**.

3. Tap **Show My Caller ID** and then disable or enable this feature.

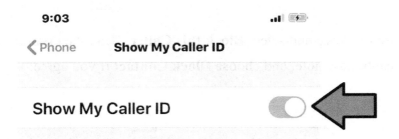

9:03 .ıl 🔋

‹ Phone   **Show My Caller ID**

Show My Caller ID   ⬭

Tip: You can have your iPhone say which contact in your

phonebook is calling you. To enable this feature, go to **Settings**
> **Phone** > **Announce Calls** > **Always**

Using the Messaging App

This app allows you to send text, image, and video messages to other SMS/MMS devices.

Starting/Managing a Conversation

1. Tap the **Messages** app from the Home screen.

2. Tap the new message icon (pen icon) located at the top right corner of the screen.

Messages

Q Search

3. Tap the **"To:"** field and type in the first letters of the recipient's name. Your device filters as you type. Then tap the required contact. Note, depending on your service provider, you can add up to 10 contacts (if not more). If you are sending the message to a phone number that is not in your address book, simply enter the phone number.

To remove a contact you have previously added, tap the

contact and tap the backspace icon ⌫ on the keyboard.

4. Tap the text entry field and write the text for your SMS/MMS.

5. To attach an image file, tap on the arrow icon  if needed and select .

Then select  and select the image you want to attach.

To write a live message, tap the digital touch icon and begin to write the message using your finger on the blackboard that appears. To change the color of the message, tap a new color. To delete the message, tap the **X** icon. When you are done, select the arrow icon to send the message.

Tap to delete the message

Pick a color

Tap to send the message

6. When you are done composing the message, tap the send icon .

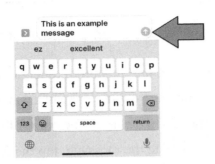

An exclamation mark ⊝ appears next to a message if the message is not sent successfully. Simply tap this exclamation mark ⊝ and select **Try again**.

To delete the message, tap and hold the message and select **More…**. Then select the delete icon 🗑 . Select **Delete Message** when prompted.

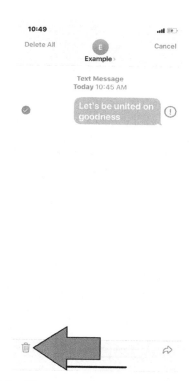

7. To send a message with a special effect, repeat steps 1 to 4 above. Then tap and hold the arrow icon and select **Screen**. Swipe the screen until you see the effect you like. Then tap the arrow icon ⬆ to send the message. To cancel the message, tap the **X** icon. Please note that message with effect is sent using iMessage. This means you may only be able to send this type of message to Apple devices. Also, wireless network or cellular data is needed to send iMessage.

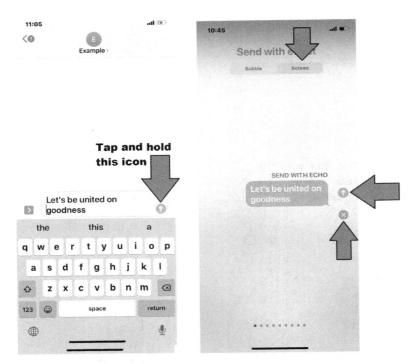

8. You can reply to a message by tapping on the message and then enter a message in the **Message** field. Tap Send icon

   when you are done. Please note that if enabled, the messages sent to other Apple devices {such as iOS devices (with iOS 5 or later), iPadOS devices, Mac computers (with OS X 10.8 or later) and Apple watches} are sent as iMessages, while non-iOS devices will receive standard text or picture messages. To learn more about iMessage, see page 128 below.

   Hint: To quickly send a prewritten reply to a message, open the Messaging app and then tap and hold a message and select a reply. You can also choose custom to enter a custom message.

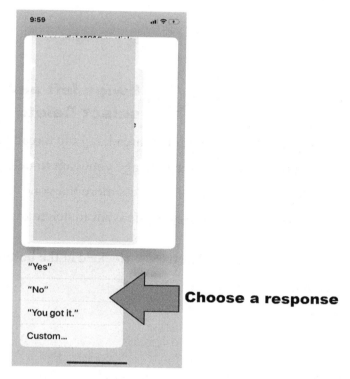

Choose a response

9. To forward a message, tap on the message to view it. Then tap and hold the message and select **More…**. Then select the forward icon ⤳ located at the bottom of the screen. Enter the desired contact and select the send icon ⬆.

10. To delete an entire message thread, swipe the thread to the left and select **Delete**. Select **Delete** again when prompted.

Swipe left and select Delete

11. To delete a single message within a thread, tap the thread to open it. Then press and hold the message you want to delete and tap on **More...**. If you want to delete more than one message, select all of the messages you want to delete by tapping them. Then select **Delete** 🗑 (located at the bottom of the screen).

Hints:

- If you are sending a message to a contact with an Apple device {such as iOS devices (with iOS 5 or later), iPadOS devices, Mac computers (with OS X 10.8 or later) and Apple watches}, the message will be sent as an iMessage. An iMessage uses Wi-Fi or cellular data to send messages. If you would like to enable/disable iMessage, from the Home screen, tap **Settings** 🔘 > **Messages.** Then tap the status switch next to **iMessages.**

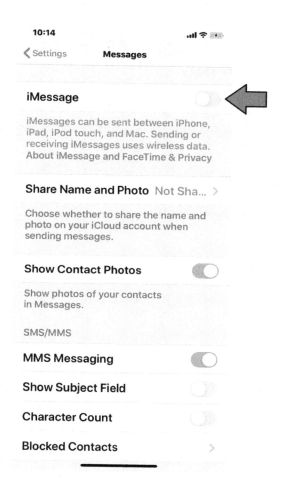

‹ Settings   **Messages**

iMessage

iMessages can be sent between iPhone,
iPad, iPod touch, and Mac. Sending or
receiving iMessages uses wireless data.
About iMessage and FaceTime & Privacy

Share Name and Photo Not Sha... **›**

Choose whether to share the name and
photo on your iCloud account when
sending messages.

Show Contact Photos

Show photos of your contacts
in Messages.

SMS/MMS

MMS Messaging

Show Subject Field

Character Count

Blocked Contacts   **›**

When using or enabling iMessage for the first time on a
carrier, you may be charged for SMS messages used to
activate iMessage.

Please note that if you enable iMessage, make sure you also
enable **Send as SMS.** This will enable you to send a message
as SMS when iMessage is unavailable. Please note that
carrier messaging rates may apply when you use this feature.

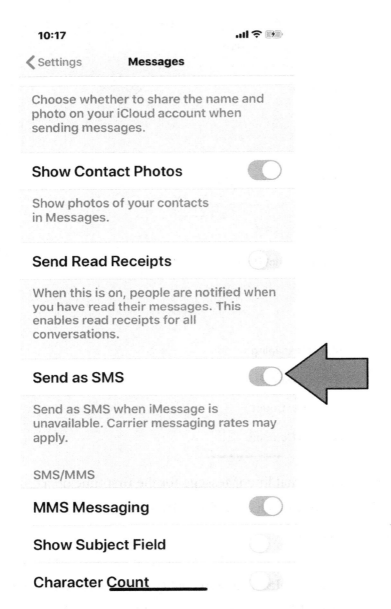

- You can know whether a message will be sent as an iMessage or as an ordinary message. To know this, check what is written on top of the screen when you are about to send the message (after selecting a contact). If **New**

iMessage is written, then an iMessage should be sent to the supported devices.

- If you receive an attachment, you can tap on the attachment to view it. To save the attachment, select and hold the attachment and choose **Save**.

- You may be able to block text messages, phone calls, e-mail or FaceTime from certain contacts/numbers. To do this, from the Home screen, tap **Settings** > **Messages** > **Blocked Contacts**. Then tap **Add New...** and select contact to block. To unblock a contact, tap **Edit** located at the top of the screen. Then tap the red minus (-) icon next to the contact you want to unblock. Thereafter, select **Unblock**.

EMAIL APP

Introduction

iPhone 11, iPhone 11 Pro and iPhone 11 Pro Max come preloaded with Mail app for sending and receiving emails and one of the things you will need to do when you start using your device is to set up an email account.

How to Add Your Email Accounts to the Mail App

You probably have many email accounts and you may wish to add these accounts to the Mail app on your device.

The email accounts you can add to the Mail app include Google Mail, Yahoo Mail, iCloud, Exchange, Outlook, among others.

To add an email account:

1. From the Home screen, tap **Settings** .
2. Scroll down and tap **Passwords & Accounts**.
3. Tap **Add Account**.
4. Tap an account and enter your email address and the password.
5. Select your preference and tap **Save**.

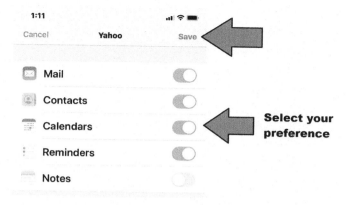

6. To add more email accounts repeat steps 1 to 5.

7. After the setup, open the Mail app from the Home screen.

Choosing a Default Email Account for Your iPhone

If you have more than one email account configured on your mobile phone, you may need to select a default email account.

1. From the Home screen, tap **Settings** .
2. Scroll down and tap **Mail**.
3. Tap **Default Account**.

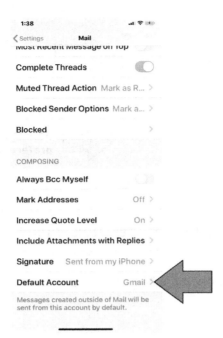

4. Tap the email account that you want to set as the default account.

How to Compose and Send an Email Using the Mail App

You can easily send an email to your friends or organization using the Mail App. In this section of the guide, we will be exploring how to compose an email and how to send an email.

To send an email:

1. From the Home screen, tap **Mail** .

2. When you open the Mail app, you will see a screen that looks like the one below.

a) **Account Name:** Tap this to get access to switch from one account to another. This is only applicable if you have multiple email accounts configured on your device. Besides, when you tap this icon, you will get access to different folders under your email account.

b) **Edit:** Tap to delete, move or mark multiple messages.

c) **Compose:** Tap to compose a new message.

d) **Filter:** Tap to filter your messages according to the read, unread, etc.

3. Tap the **compose icon** (the pen icon) 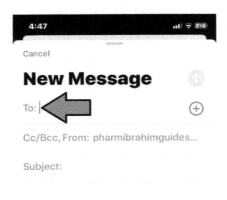 .

4. Tap the field next to **"To:"** and type in the email address of the recipient.

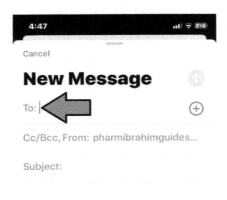

5. To send a copy to another person, tap **CC/Bcc** field and type the person's email address in the **Cc/Bcc** field.

Tip: Cc means Carbon Copy. If you use the Cc option to send a message to multiple recipients, all the recipients will see the message and all other email addresses that have received the message. On the other hand, Bcc stands for Blind Carbon Copy. If you use the Bcc option to send a message to multiple recipients, all the recipients will see the message, but will not see other email addresses that have received the message.

6. Tap **Subject** and key in the required subject.

7. Tap the text input field and write the text for your email.

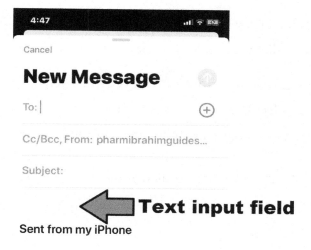

8. To access more info, tap and hold a blank area or a word in the message field and then choose an option.

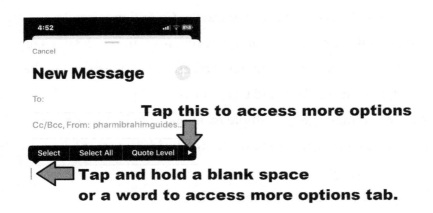

To access more options while using the options tab, tap the

right-facing arrow ▶.

To bold, italicize or underline a text, tap and hold the text and

tap the right-facing arrow ▶ (if needed). Then tap the **BIU**

icon and select bold, italic or underline.

9. When you are satisfied with the message and you are ready

to send it, tap **Send** ⬆ located at the top of the Mail app

screen.

Tip: If you're writing a message and want to finish it later, tap **Cancel** located at the top of the screen, then tap **Save Draft**. To get it back, touch and hold the Compose button ⬜ . Alternatively, open the Mail app, and swipe right from the left edge of the screen.

Attaching a File

You can insert an attachment into your message. To do this, tap and hold a blank area in the message field and then tap the right-facing arrow.

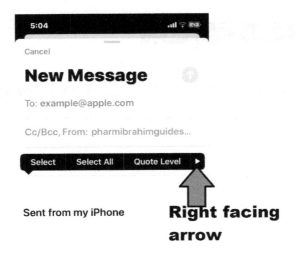

Sent from my iPhone   **Right facing arrow**

Tap **Add document** or **Insert Photo or Video**. Then locate and tap on the file you want to attach.

Tip: You can group those emails with attachment together under a folder. To do this:

- Open the Mail app and tap **Mailboxes.**

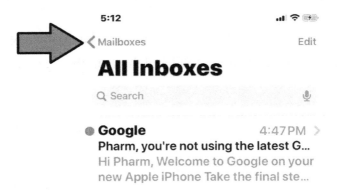

- Tap **Edit**.

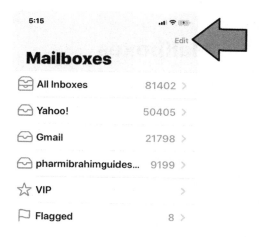

- Select **Attachment**.

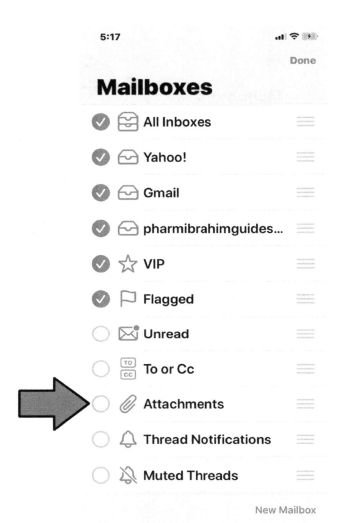

- Tap **Done**.

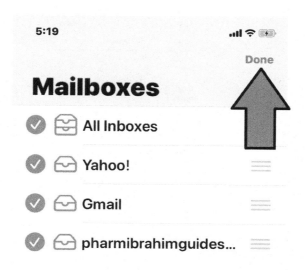

To access the newly created Attachment folder, simply open the Mail app and swipe right from the left edge of the screen.

Managing a Received Email

One of the most important functions of any email app is the ability to receive incoming messages. By default, the Mail app searches for new messages and alerts you when there is one.

New messages are either stored in Inbox or Junk/Spam folder and these are the places to check if you are expecting an email.

To read a message or manage a received message:

- Tap on the subject of the message to open the message text in the preview pane.

- Unread messages will appear with blue badges.

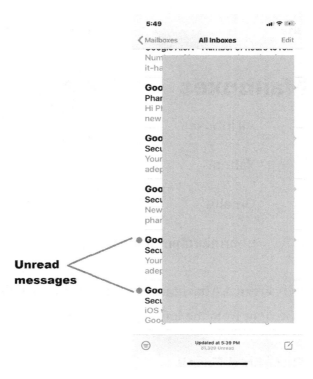

Unread messages

Updated at 5:39 PM
81,309 Unread

- The attachment icon (a paperclip icon) means that a message has an attachment.

- To change the email account/inbox view, continue to swipe right from the left edge of the screen until you see **Mailboxes**. Then tap the account you want to view.

Edit

Mailboxes

📬 All Inboxes	81404	>
📬 Yahoo!	50406	>
📬 Gmail	21799	>
📬 pharmibrahimguides...	9199	>
☆ VIP		>
▭ Flagged	8	>
📎 Attachments	14	>

- To reply to a message, tap ↩ and then tap **Reply**. When you tap the reply button, a new window appears. This window is similar to what appears when you tap on new email button but with a slight difference. This window already contains the recipient's name and the subject.

- To forward a message, tap ↩ and then tap **Forward.** Use this option to send a copy of an email in your inbox to your friends or associates. When you tap on the Forward button, a message window with a subject line preceded by "Fwd:" appears. The original subject and text are also included. In addition, you will have the option to fill in the email address of the person to whom you are sending the message.

- To archive an email, while viewing the message in the list view, swipe the email from right to left. When you archive a message, it is removed from your inbox and placed in **Archive** folder. This makes your inbox less cluttered. To access Archive folder, open the Mail app, and swipe right from the left edge of the screen.

Tip: When you tap the more options icon ↰ found at the bottom of the screen when reading a message, you will get access to the following options:

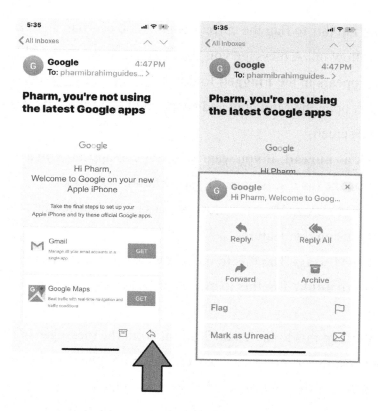

1. **Reply:** Tap this to reply to a message.

2. **Reply all**: If an email is sent to more than one person, you can tap **Reply all** to reply to all those who have received the message.

3. **Forward**: Select this option to forward a message to another person.

4. **Archive:** Tap this to archive a message. When you archive a message, it is removed from your inbox and placed in the **Archive** folder. This makes your inbox less cluttered. To access the Archive folder, open the Mail app, and swipe right from the left edge of the screen.

5. **Flag**: tap this to flag the current email. You can flag an email for follow up. A message you flag remains in your inbox but also appears in the **Flagged** folder. To access the Flagged folder, open the Mail app, and swipe right from the left edge of the screen.

6. **Mark as unread**: If you want a message to appear with a blue badge (as if it is unread), tap "Mark as Unread".

7. **Move Message**: You can move a message to a different folder using this feature.

8. **Trash Message** Tap this to move a message to the trash bin.

9. **Move to Junk**: Tap this to move a message to the Junk folder.

10. **Mute**: Tap this to mute notifications from the messages in a conversation. If there is a busy email thread, you can reduce disturbances by muting notifications from the thread. You can customize what the Mail app does with emails you have muted. To do this, from the Home screen, go to **Settings** and select **Mail**. Scroll down and select **Muted Thread Action**. Then choose an option.

11. **Notify Me**: If you want to get notified when there is a reply to an email or thread, select "Notify me".

12. **Print**: Use this option to print an email.

Please note that some options discussed above may not appear for some emails.

To close the more options dialogue box, tap the **X** icon.

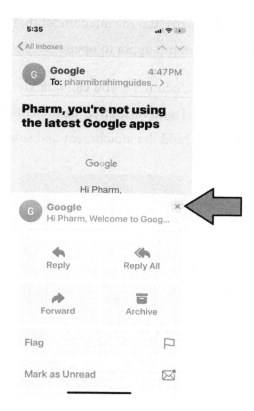

How to Open and Save an Attachment in the Mail App

The email with an attachment will have a paper clip icon displayed next to the address of the sender when you check your message inbox.

To open an attachment:

1. Tap the message that has the attachment, as indicated by a paper clip.

2. When the message opens, tap the attachment that you want to download. If needed, tap it again to open.

3. If the attachment is a document, you can quickly view it using "Quick Look." To do this, after the attachment is downloaded, tap and hold the attachment and select **Quick Look**.

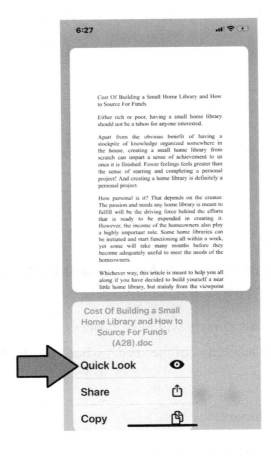

4. To save an attachment, tap and hold the attachment and select **Share**. Then scroll up and select **Save to Files**. Then

choose **On My iPhone** or **iCloud Drive** and select **Save** found at the top of the screen.

5. Downloaded attachments are found in **Files** app. To access

the **Files** app, from the Home screen, tap on **Files** .

Please note that if the attachment you downloaded is PDF, you may need to check the **Books** app on the Home screen to access it. If the attachment is an image or video, go to **Photos** app to locate.

Tip: To see only messages with attachments, tap the Filter Messages button ⬚ (located at the bottom left of the screen) to turn on filtering, then tap **Filtered by** and select **Only Mail with Attachments**.

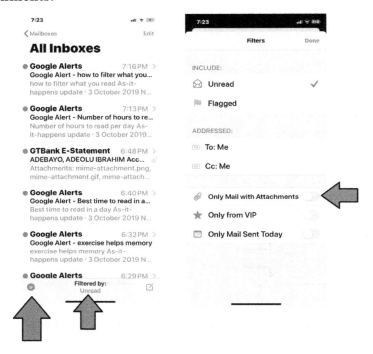

Managing the Email Settings

1. From the Home screen, tap **Settings** .
2. Scroll down and tap **Mail**.
3. Tap an option to customize.

Deleting an Email Account

1. From the Home screen, tap **Settings** .
2. Scroll down and tap **Passwords & Accounts**.
3. Tap the required email account.
4. Tap **Delete Account**.

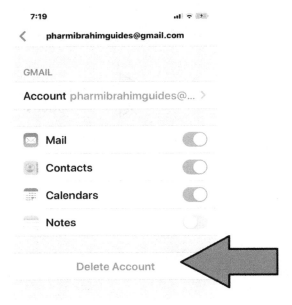

5. Tap **Delete from My iPhone**.

How to Change the Default Email Signature in Email App

You can use the Signature setting to tell the Mail app what signature to include in a message.

1. From the Home screen, tap **Settings** .
2. Scroll down and tap **Mail**.
3. Scroll down and tap **Signature**.
4. Tap the current signature and adjust it as you like. When you

   are done, tap the back icon located at the top of the

   screen.

Note: An email signature is a text that appears by default after the body of your message. You may set your email signature to be your name or your brand.

Personal Information

Contacts

This app allows you to create and manage a list of your personal or business contacts. You can save names, mobile phone numbers, home phone numbers, email addresses, and more.

Creating a Contact

1. While on the Home screen, tap on **Contacts** 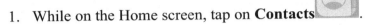.
2. Tap on **Contacts** app.
3. Tap on + located at the upper right corner of the screen.

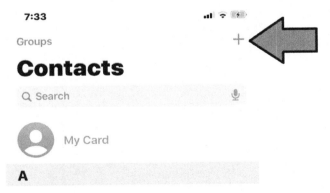

4. Fill in the details by tapping on each item on the screen and entering the appropriate information.

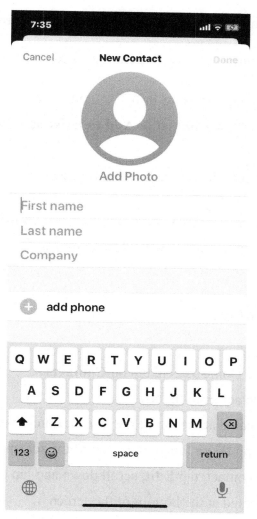

5. Scroll down to add more details.

6. When you are done, tap **Done** located at the top of the screen.

Hint: To search for a contact, open the contact app and tap the search bar located at the top of the screen. Then start typing a name; the list filters as you write.

You can add a recent caller to your Contacts. To do this, from the

Home screen, tap **Phone** 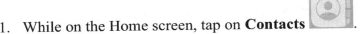, tap **Recents** (located at the bottom of

the screen), and then tap the More Info button next to the

number. Tap **Create New Contact** or **Add to Existing Contact**, and

follow the prompts.

Tip: To change the default storage location for newly added

contacts, go to **Settings** > **Contacts** > **Default Account**. Then

select where you want to store newly added contacts.

Managing a Contact

1. While on the Home screen, tap on **Contacts** .

2. Tap on a contact from the list.

3. Tap **Edit** located at the top of the screen. Enter the new

   details and tap **Done** found at the top of the screen.

4. To delete a contact, tap **Edit**, scroll down and tap on **Delete**

   Contact located at the bottom of the screen.

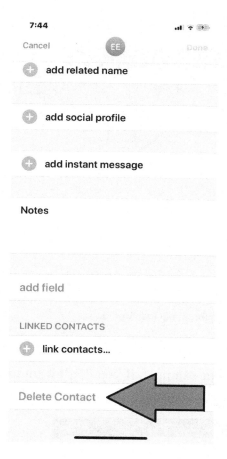

Tip: You can quickly hide all your contacts. To do this, open
Contact app. Tap **Groups** located at the top of the screen.

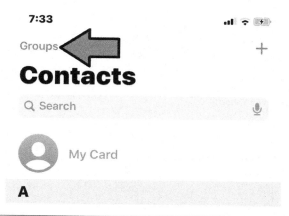

Then select **Hide All Contacts** and tap **Done** to save the changes.

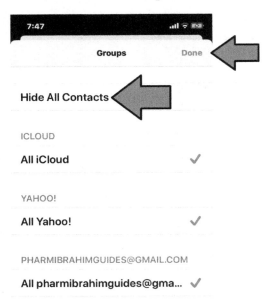

To prevent contacts from an account from being shown, simply unselect the account. For example, if you don't want to see contacts from **All iCloud**, make sure it is not selected.

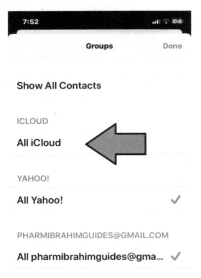

To unhide your contacts, tap **Groups** again (found at the top of the screen) and tap **Show All Contacts** and then tap **Done**.

Adding a Contact to Favorites List

1. From the Home screen, tap on **Phone**  app.
2. Tap the Favorites icon.
3. Tap the plus sign (+) icon located at the top of the screen.

No Favorites

4. Tap a contact to add to Favorites and select whether you are adding **Message, Call** or **Mail**.

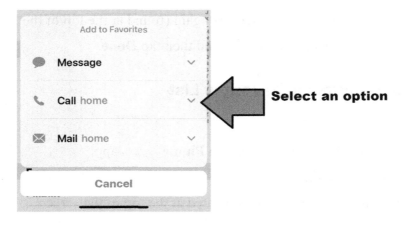

Select an option

5. To remove a contact from the Favorites tab, swipe the contact towards left from the right edge of the screen. Alternatively, tap **Edit** located at the top of the screen and then tap the red minus (-) icon next to the contact you want to remove. Then select **Delete.**

Linking Two Contacts

1. While on the Home screen, select the **Contacts** app.
2. Tap the contact you want to link.
3. Tap **Edit** located at the top of the screen.
4. Scroll down and tap **Link Contacts...**
5. Tap the required contact.
6. Tap **Link** located at the top of the screen.
7. Tap **Done** found at the top of the screen to save the changes.

8. To unlink contacts, tap the contact, tap **Edit** located at the top of the screen. Scroll down to the bottom of the screen and tap the red minus icon next to the contact you want to unlink.

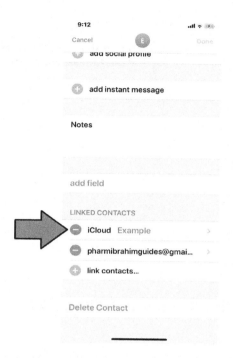

Thereafter, tap **Unlink.** Tap **Done** found at the top of the screen to save the changes. Please note that unlinking a contact does not delete the contact.

Linking two contacts is important if you have separate entries for the same contact from different social networking services or email accounts.

Hint: To customize the Contact app, from the Home screen, tap on

Settings , tap **Contacts** and then select an option.

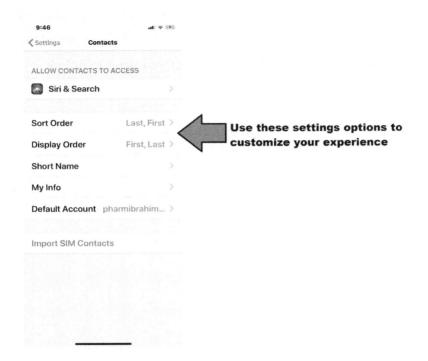

ALLOW CONTACTS TO ACCESS

Siri & Search   ›

Sort Order   Last, First ›

Display Order   First, Last ›

Short Name   ›

My Info   ›

Default Account pharmibrahim... ›

Import SIM Contacts

Use these settings options to customize your experience

Importing/Exporting Contacts from One Account to Another

If you have your contacts backup on your email account, you can link this email account to your iPhone so that the contacts can be automatically added to your Contacts app.

1. From the Home screen, tap **Settings** .

2. Scroll down and tap **Passwords & Accounts**.

3. Tap **Add Account**.

4. Select an account and follow the onscreen instructions to link your account and sync your contacts. During the account-linking process, please make sure **Contacts** is enabled.

Make sure "Contacts" is selected

Tip: If you don't enable Contact during the account setup and you wish to enable it at any other time, go to **Settings** 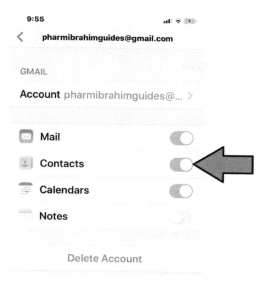 > **Passwords & Accounts**. Then tap the account you want to extract the contacts from. Thereafter, tap the status switch next to **Contacts** to enable contact syncing.

Accessibility Features – The Special Features for Easy Usage

Accessibility features let you customize your device to suit your needs. Besides, they also provide you with the opportunity to control your phone in a special way.

Tip: To access the Accessibility features, from the Home screen, tap Settings 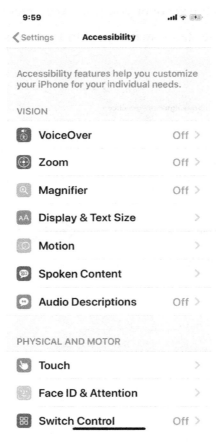, and tap **Accessibility.**

Some of the Accessibility options are discussed below:

1. **VoiceOver:** This feature reads what you do on the screen aloud making it possible to interact with your device even if you have difficulty seeing the screen. VoiceOver tells you about each item you select by enclosing the item and describing it. You can enable VoiceOver by tapping the VoiceOver status switch.

When VoiceOver is enabled, you will need to control your screen in a special way to get results.

Basically, you will need to tap the screen to hear the items on the screen or select items. To access the selected item or perform a specific action on the item, double-tap the screen.

To learn more about VoiceOver, simply read the onscreen instructions that appear when you tap on VoiceOver.

2. **Zoom:** This feature allows you to zoom in/out items on the screen. You can enable Zoom by tapping the Zoom status switch. When Zoom is enabled, you can double-tap the screen with three fingers to zoom.

In addition, you can limit the maximum magnification by adjusting the slider under the **Maximum Zoom Level**.

- Drag three fingers to move around the screen
- Double-tap three fingers and drag to change zoom

Follow Focus

Smart Typing

Smart Typing will switch to Window Zoom when a keyboard appears and move the Window so that text is zoomed, but the keyboard is not.

Keyboard Shortcuts   On ›

Zoom Controller   Off ›

Zoom Region   Full Screen Zoom ›

Zoom Filter   None ›

MAXIMUM ZOOM LEVEL

5.0x

3. **Magnifier:** When this option is enabled, you can use your iPhone to magnify items near you just as you do with a magnifying glass. When enabled, triple-click the side button to launch the Magnifier. **Tip**: Magnifier is like using your iPhone like a magnifying lens. To return to the Home screen after using Magnifier, swipe up from the bottom of the screen.

4. Display & Text Size: This option allows you to tweak color and font on the screen of your device so as to make the screen easier to read.

5. Motion: When this option is enabled, motion of the user interface, including the parallax effect of icons and related settings may be reduced.

6. Spoken content: This option allows you to customize speech-related options.

7. Audio Description: When this option is enabled, your iPhone may provide an audio descriptions of video scenes for videos that include audio descriptions.

8. Touch: Use this feature to customize how the screen responds to touches. With this feature, you can configure the iPhone to respond only to touches of a certain duration.

9. Face ID & Attention: This feature includes settings related to Face ID, screen brightness, volume controls of alerts, etc.

10. Switch Control: This feature is particularly good for those with motor impairment. Switch Control lets you control your phone using a connected physical switch, your phone screen, or phone camera. I will advise you don't tamper with the **Switch Control** unless you know much about it. To disable the Switch Control, triple-click the side button.

11. Voice Control: This option allows you to control your phone using your voice

12. Side Button: Use this option to manage how the Side button behaves.

13. **Apple TV Remote**: Use this option to manage Apple TV Remote settings.

14. **Keyboard**: Use this tab to customize virtual keyboard-related settings.

15. **Hearing Devices**: Use this tab to connect hearing aid to your iPhone.

16. **Audio/Visual:** This feature allows you to adjust the sound from the left and right channels so that you can hear the sound from your iPhone with either ear.

If you want your device to use LED Flash for alerts, enable **LED Flash for Alerts**. Please note that this might only work if the ring switch is set to silent. Ring switch is the button next to the volumes key at the side of your phone.

17. **Subtitles & Captioning:** Use this tab to customize subtitles & captioning related settings.

17. **Guided Access:** This option allows you to restrict your access to some apps/tasks on your phone for a particular time.

18. **Siri**: Use this option to control how Siri behaves when you press the side key.

19. **Accessibility Shortcuts**: This option lets you turn the accessibility features you use most on and off by triple-clicking the side button.

Hints: Interestingly, Apple includes descriptions under many Accessibility options. You can read these descriptions to know how to tweak them.

TOOLS

Lower Power Mode

Low Power Mode allows you to conserve battery and use your phone for longer hours. Please note that some processes may behave unusually when this mode is enabled. For example, your iPhone may perform some tasks more slowly when this feature is enabled.

To enable Low Power Mode:

1. From the Home screen, tap **Settings** .
2. Tap **Battery**.
3. Tap the indicator switch next to **Low Power Mode**.

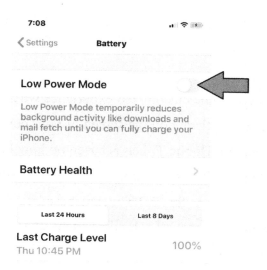

Tip: Are you worrying that your iPhone is not holding charge? If yes, check the battery health to know if the battery is good. To do this, go to **Settings** 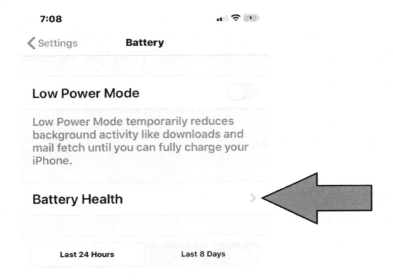 > **Battery** > **Battery Health**. This is one of the things to look for when buying a used phone.

7:08

〈 Settings   **Battery**

Low Power Mode

Low Power Mode temporarily reduces background activity like downloads and mail fetch until you can fully charge your iPhone.

Battery Health   〉

Last 24 Hours   Last 8 Days

Haptic Touch

Haptic Touch gives you some customized experience when you press and hold some items firmly on the screen of your device. This is similar to 3D Touch but Haptic Touch is based on how long you press and hold an item while 3D Touch is based on how soft/hard you press an item. This means that 3D Touch is based on the force applied when pressing an item while Haptic Touch is based on the length of time of pressing an item.

- **Using Haptic Touch on the Home Screen:** To use Haptic Touch on the Home screen, press and hold an app icon firmly to bring out the app shortcuts. The app shortcut for the message app is shown below.

Please note that if you press and hold the button for a longer period, the apps will begin to shake instead, and you will not be able to access the Haptic Touch options.

- **Using Haptic Touch in the Mail App:** To use Haptic Touch in the Mail app, press and hold an email message for one to two seconds to preview the email then swipe up to bring up more options (like the one shown below).

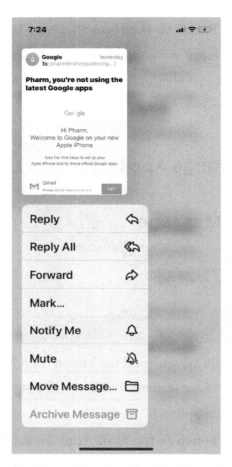

- **Using Haptic Touch in the Contact App:** To use Haptic Touch in contact app, press and hold a contact firmly to bring up options.

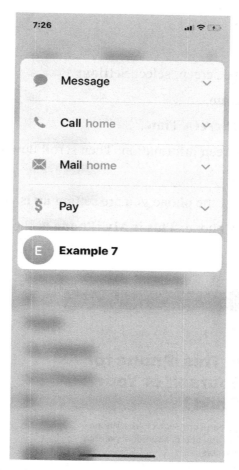

To exit Haptic Touch options, simply tap outside the options.

Being Productive with Screen Time

Screen Time allows you to use your phone productively. This app allows you to know how you have used your phone in a day/week. It allows you to see the number of hours spent on each app. Interestingly, you can limit the time spent on each app using this app.

To use Screen Time:

1. From the Home screen, select **Settings** .

2. Tap **Screen Time**.

3. Tap **Turn On Screen Time**.

4. Read the on-screen information. Then scroll down and select **Continue**.

5. Choose whether the phone you are setting up is your iPhone or your child's phone. **This is My iPhone** is chosen in this example.

6. The summary of how you use your phone is shown in a chart. To get a detailed usage analysis, tap on **See All Activity**.

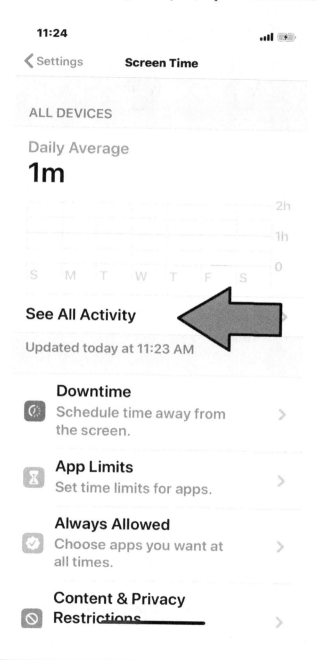

You can view the activities on a daily or weekly basis.

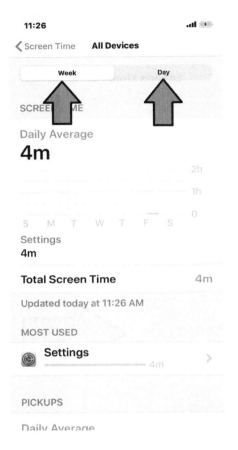

Using a Screen Time Passcode

You can use a passcode to protect Screen Time settings and allow for more time when limits expire. To do this:

1. From the Home screen, select **Settings** .
2. Tap **Screen Time**.
3. Scroll down and select **Use Screen Time Code**. Enter passcode and enter it again to confirm.

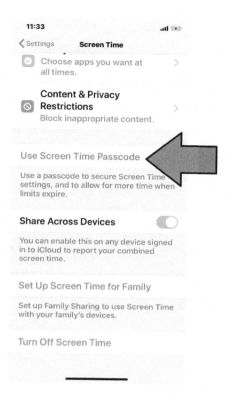

Please note that if you have already set up a Screen Time passcode, you will see **Change Screen Time Passcode** instead.

Using Downtime

You can use Screen Time to restrict the amount of time you spend using your phone. To do this:

1. From the Home screen, select **Settings** 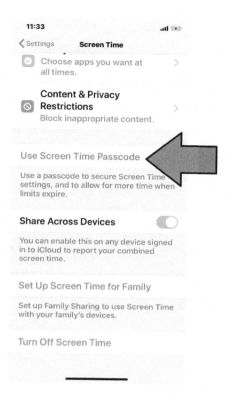.
2. Tap **Screen Time**.
3. Tap on **Downtime**. Enter your Screen Time passcode if needed.
4. Tap the status switch next **Downtime**.

5. To use Downtime every day, select **Every Day**. If you want to use Downtime in a customized way, select **Customize Days** and tap a day to enable or disable Downtime for the day. For example, to enable Downtime for Sunday, tap on **Sunday** and select the switch next to **Sunday** to disable or enable Downtime for this day.

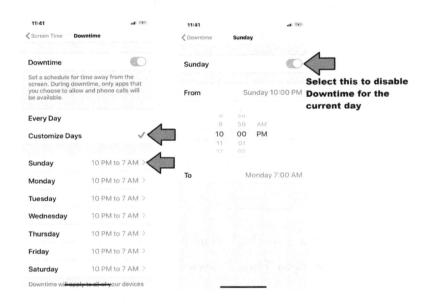

Choosing the Apps that Are Available During Downtime

You can choose those apps you want to access when Downtime is running. To do this:

1. From the Home screen, Select Settings .
2. Tap **Screen Time**.
3. Select **Always Allowed**.

4. Tap the plus + icon next to the apps you want to be able to access. To remove an app, tap the minus icon next to the app and select **Remove**.

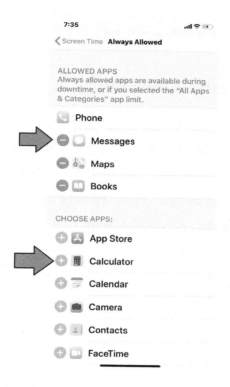

Using the Screen Time to Restrict Actions on Your Phone

You can use Screen Time to restrict actions or block inappropriate content from being shown to you.

To do this:

1. From the Home screen, select **Settings** .
2. Tap **Screen Time**.
3. Select **Content & Privacy Restrictions**.

4. Tap the status switch next to **Content & Privacy Privacy**
    Restrictions.

5. Tap on **Content Restrictions**. Carefully go through each tab
    and choose an appropriate option. For example, if you want a
    clean result to be shown to you when you access the Book
    app, tap on **Books** and select **Clean**.

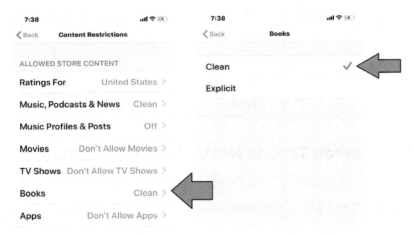

Besides, you can limit the web content view on your phone
by tapping on Web Content and then choosing **Limit Adult**
Websites or **Allowed Websites Only**.

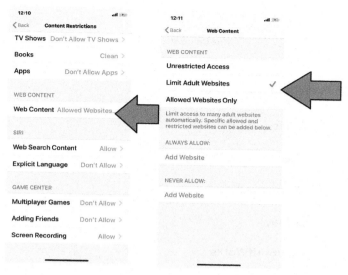

If you choose *Allowed Websites Only*, you will able to
choose those websites that can be accessed on the phone by
tapping on **Add Website**.

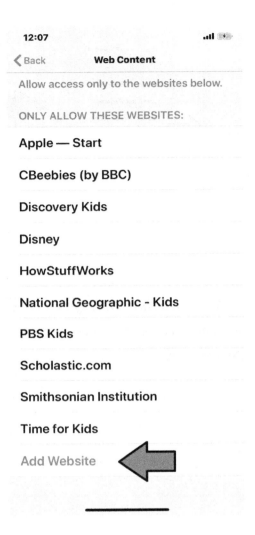

Tip: You can use Screen Time to prevent people from installing or deleting apps on your device. **To do this:**

1. From the Home screen, Select Settings 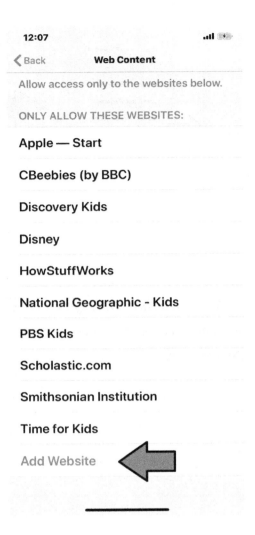.
2. Tap **Screen Time**.
3. Select **Content & Privacy Restrictions**.
4. Tap **iTunes & App Store Purchases**.

5. Tap on **Installing Apps** or **Deleting Apps** and choose an appropriate option.

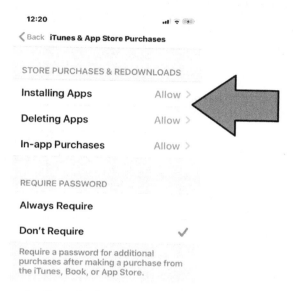

Preventing people from being able to install apps on your phone makes it harder for people to have a backdoor to content you will not allow ordinarily.

Do Not Disturb

If you don't want to be disturbed by calls or notifications, you can set your mobile phone to be silent for a specified amount of time.

1. From the Home screen, tap **Settings** .
2. Tap **Do Not Disturb**.

3. To turn on/off **Do Not Disturb,** tap the status switch next to **Do Not Disturb**. Please note that when Do Not Disturb is enabled, calls and alerts that arrive while your iPhone is locked will be silenced.

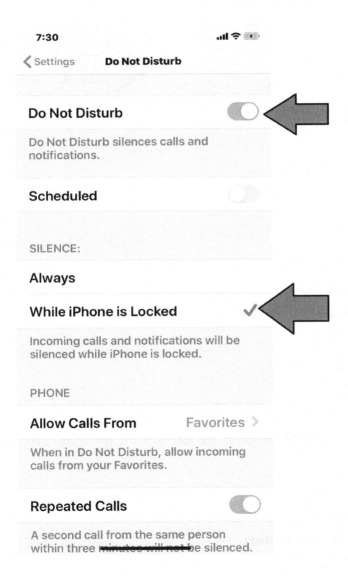

4. To set the time when Do Not Disturb will be active, tap the status switch next to **Schedule.**

5. Tap **From** and scroll to the time you would like Do Not Disturb to begin.

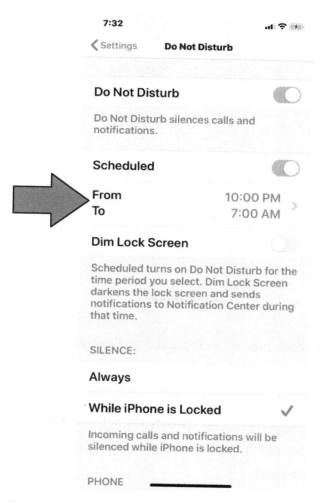

6. Tap **To** and scroll to the time you would like Do Not Disturb to end.

7. Tap the back button ❮ located at the top of the screen to save changes.

8. Tap **Always** if you want to set your mobile phone to silent mode permanently. Tap **Only while iPhone is locked** if you want to set your mobile phone to a silent mode only when the phone is locked.

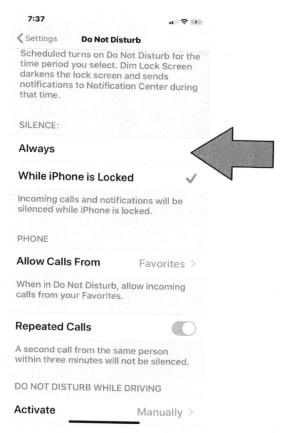

9. Tap **Allow Calls From** to choose who is able to call you while Do Not Disturb is turned on. You may choose favorite if you want to receive calls from only your favorites when Do Not Disturb is enabled. To know more about Favorites, please go to page 161.

10. To allow your phone to ring aloud (the second time) when the same person calls you two times within three minutes, tap the status switch next to **Repeated Calls.**

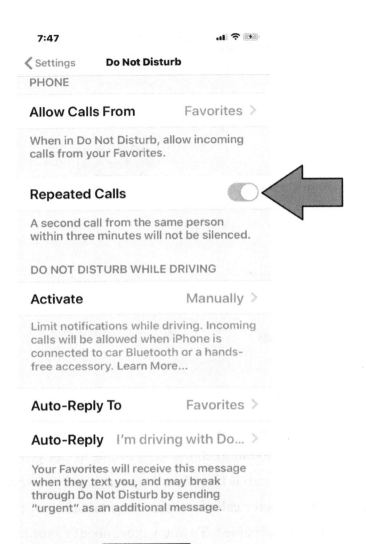

PHONE

Allow Calls From   Favorites ›

When in Do Not Disturb, allow incoming
calls from your Favorites.

Repeated Calls

A second call from the same person
within three minutes will not be silenced.

DO NOT DISTURB WHILE DRIVING

Activate   Manually ›

Limit notifications while driving. Incoming
calls will be allowed when iPhone is
connected to car Bluetooth or a hands-
free accessory. Learn More...

Auto-Reply To   Favorites ›

Auto-Reply I'm driving with Do... ›

Your Favorites will receive this message
when they text you, and may break
through Do Not Disturb by sending
"urgent" as an additional message.

11. To turn **Do Not Disturb** off, swipe down from the top-right

edge of the screen to access Control Center and then tap **Do**

Not Disturb icon   .

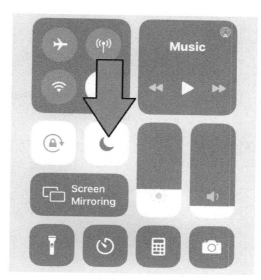

Tip: You can automatically enable Do Not Disturb while driving.

Simply go to **Settings** > **Do Not Disturb**. Then scroll down to **Do Not Disturb While Driving** and select **Activate**. Then choose **Automatically**.

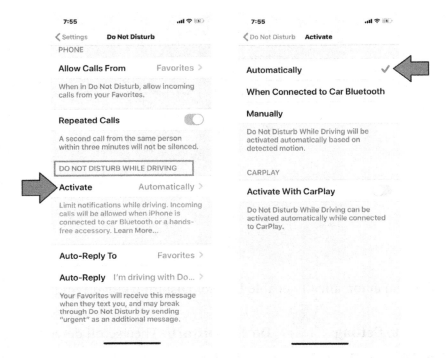

Please note that people in your Favorites list may get an automatic response when they text you while you are driving and Do Not Disturb is switched on.

Creating Schedules and More with the Calendar

Your phone provides you with the **Calendar** app to help you organize your schedules and tasks more conveniently and effectively. You can create schedules and add events.

Creating an event

1. From the Home screen, tap on **Calendar** .

2. When using the Calendar app for the first time, follow the onscreen instructions to set it up.

3. Tap on + located at the upper right corner of the screen.

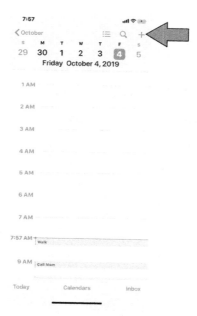

4. To set the start and end date/time of the event, tap the on-screen date/time and adjust them accordingly. If the event is an all-day event, tap the status switch next to **All-day** to activate it. When you activate all-day, you would not be able to set a specific time for your event. To learn more about all-day event, see page 196.

5. Fill in other details by tapping on each item on the screen.

6. When you are done, tap **Add**.

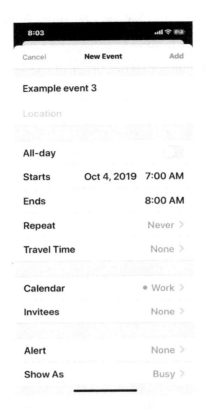

Editing and deleting an event

1. From the Home screen, tap on **Calendar** 4 .

2. Tap the event date and then tap on the event you want to delete.

3. Tap **Edit** located at the top of the screen and make necessary corrections. Tap **Done** to save the changes.

4. To delete an event, tap **Delete Event** found at the bottom of the screen.

Example event 3

Friday, Oct 4, 2019
from 7 AM to 8 AM

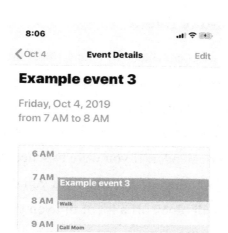

Calendar	● Work ❯
Alert	None ❯

Delete Event

Understanding All-day Event

All-day event is a type of event that will take a lot of hours to be completed. For example, if an event will begin by 9 a.m. and finish by 6 p.m., this type of event should be categorized as an all-day event. This would make it easier to see all other schedules happening during this time on your calendar. If you were to schedule an event between 9 a.m. and 6 p.m. on your calendar (and you don't select it as an all-day event), it will block off a lot of time on your calendar. It may also overshadow other concurrent events.

To make an event an all-day event, please go to step 4 under **Creating an Event** (see page 192-194).

Changing your calendar view and viewing events

1. From the Home screen, tap on **Calendar** .

2. Tap the small back arrow next to the Month to change from day view to month view or from month view to year view.

3. To access day view and see your events, tap **Today** located at the bottom of the screen. Then tap the menu icon to view events for the day.

Hint: To search for items on your calendar, tap the search button (lens icon) and begin to type a keyword.

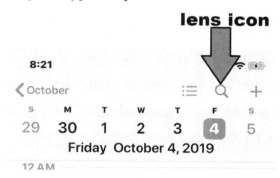

In addition, you can view a weekly calendar by rotating your iPhone sideways and then tapping on **Week**. Please note that screen rotation has to be enabled to achieve this. To enable screen rotation, swipe down from the right edge of the screen and select ⟲ .

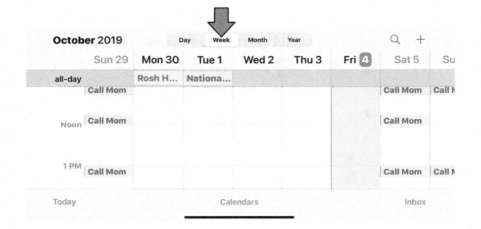

Inviting People to Your Events

If you have an upcoming event, you can invite people to it using the Calendar app. To do this:

1. From the Home screen, tap on **Calendar** .
2. Tap the plus icon "+" at the upper right side of the screen.
3. To set the start and end date/time of the event, tap onscreen date/time and adjust them accordingly. If the event is an all-day event, tap the status switch next to **All-day** to activate it. When you activate all-day, you would not be able to set a specific time. To learn more about an all-day event, please go to page 196.
4. To enter a title for your event, tap "Title" located at the top of the screen and enter a title.
5. To invite people to your event, tap **Invitees** and type the name of those you are inviting. The list filters as you type. To select any suggested name, tap it. You can also enter the

email address(es) if you don't have the contact(s) of those you are inviting. Simply enter the email address and tap *"return"* on the virtual keyboard. Tap **Done** (found at the top of the screen). Tap the back icon next to **New Event** to continue editing the event.

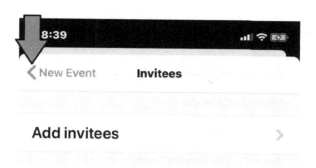

6. Fill in other details.
7. When you are done, tap **Add** (located at the top of the screen).

Generally, Apple will send out email invitations to the invited guests/people after you save the event. The invitees will have the opportunity to respond to the request through their emails.

Tip: To see the people coming to your event, simply open the Calendar app and tap on the event. Then tap on **Invitees**.

Tip: To customize calendar settings, from the Home screen, tap **Settings**, tap **Calendar** and choose an option.

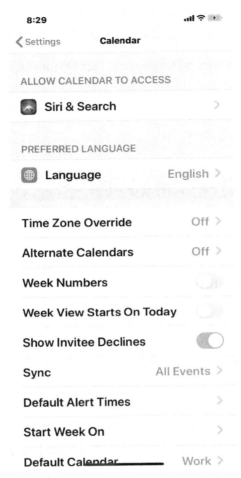

Tip: If you want your Google Calendar to be sync with your iPhone,

go to **Settings** > **Passwords & Accounts**. Then tap your

Google account and tap the status switch next to **Calendars** to

enable calendar syncing.

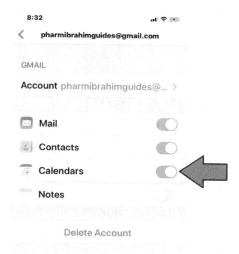

You can also use this above method to sync calendars from other accounts.

In the tip above, please note that I assumed that you have already linked your Google account, if you have not, then go to **Settings** > **Passwords & Accounts**. Then tap **Add Accounts** and follow the prompts.

Using the Camera

iPhone 11, iPhone 11 Pro and iPhone 11 Pro Max come with rear-facing cameras, front-facing camera and LED flash. With these cameras, you can capture a photo or record a video.

Note: The memory capacity of the picture taken may differ depending on the settings, shooting scene and shooting conditions.

> **To Capture a photo**

1. From the Home screen tap **Camera** .

2. If necessary, swipe the screen to **PHOTO**

3. Aim the lens at the subject and make any necessary adjustments. To focus on any part of the screen, tap that part of the screen.

3. If the front-facing camera is in use, tap **front-facing/rear-facing**

icon to switch to the rear-facing camera and vice versa.

4. To zoom in, place two fingers on the screen and spread them apart. Do the reverse to zoom out.

5. To add a filter, tap the filter icon. Then tap the filter you would like to use. If the filter icon is not showing, tap the hidden icons button found at the top of the screen to bring it into view.

6. Tap on **camera button** when you are done adjusting the settings.

To customize camera settings:

1. From the Home screen, tap **Settings** .

2. Scroll down and tap **Camera**.

3. Tap an option.

Hint: Camera settings consist of quite a number of features, you may not need to touch some of the features. In fact, the default settings are enough for many users.

Using the Live Photo Option

You can use live photos to capture a moving scene or moving object. For example, you can use the live photo to capture a moving car.

To do this:

1. Open the Camera app.
2. Tap on the hidden icons button to bring the live photo icon into view .
3. Aim the lens of your camera at the target and press the shutter button .
4. Then tap on the preview of the photo you just took and select **Edit**. Tap on Live icon found at the bottom of the screen.
5. Select the best image from the frame and choose **Make Key Photo**. Tap **Done** to save the changes.

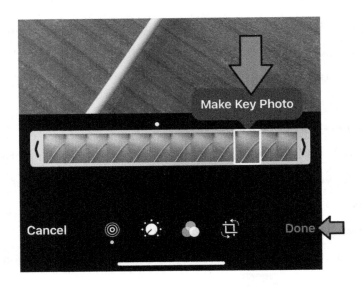

Using Photo Timer

Photo timer allows you to tell your device when to take a picture automatically.

To use this option:

- From the Home screen tap **Camera** .

- Tap the timer icon ![timer], choose 3s or 10s and then tap the shutter button ![shutter] .

- Then wait for the camera to take the picture after the countdown.

Recording a Video

1. From the Home screen tap **Camera** .

2. Swipe the screen until **Video** is selected.

3. Tap the **video button** .

4. When done with the recording, tap the **video button** again.

5. To view your recorded videos, go to the Photos app.

Tip: To delete an image, from the Home Screen, go to **Photos**, tap

the image you want to delete and tap the delete icon located at the bottom of the screen.

To edit an image, tap the image, then tap **Edit** and pick an editing tool. When you are done editing, tap **Done** located at the bottom of the screen.

Getting Productive with the Camera

Many people use the camera of their phone just to take pictures, but don't know that they can be using their phone camera for more productive tasks.

Interestingly, your device features powerful cameras that transform the way you use a camera. In this section, we will be exploring ways we can be more productive with our phone cameras.

Ways to be more productive with your phone camera are mentioned below:

- **Use your phone camera as a scanner for your documents**

You probably have many documents that are very important to you. Why don't you find time to take the pictures of all these documents and save them on your phone or have them stored in the cloud. There are times that you would want to check something in a document, but you are not at home. Saving the pictures of your documents on your phone should help you in times like this. In addition, saving the pictures of your documents on your phone will save you time and stress because you have access to them on the go.

Top document scanners include **Microsoft Office Lens** and **Adobe Scan**. You can download these apps from Google Play store.

- **Take pictures of the natural environment like a waterfall and natural vegetation**

According to reports, looking at the pictures of natural environments like waterfalls and natural vegetations gives people pleasure and serves as coolness to the eyes. In addition, it helps you appreciate the beautiful works of the Almighty God.

- **Declutter your life**

Do you know that you can use the camera of your phone to declutter your life? You probably have many hand-written documents, business cards, to-do lists, etc. lying all over the place in your home.

You can take the picture of these notes so that you can remove them from your house and give them to appropriate waste recycling companies. This will create more space in your house and give you more visual ventilation.

I would advise you properly label the pictures of your hand-written documents, business cards, to-do list, etc. to help you easily find them in the future. In addition, you can consider saving the pictures of your hand-written documents, business cards, to-do list, etc. on *Evernote*. I suggest Evernote because it gives you the opportunity to search texts inside images.

- **Use your camera as a barcode and QR (quick response) code scanner**

Barcode and QR code are machine-readable codes that are used to store information. Barcode is linear or one dimensional in nature. It basically looks like a cluster of parallel lines. On the other hand, QR code is two dimensional in nature. An example of a QR code is shown below. Interestingly, your iPhone is capable of reading QR codes and barcodes using QR codes and barcode scanner apps. Many of us still take the long path of entering texts or links when we can get the same result by scanning barcode or QR code.

Example of a QR code

You can install a QR code/barcode scanner from Apple store. Simply search for *barcode scanner* or *QR and barcode scanner*.

- **Take the pictures of notes in meetings and lectures instead of writing them**

Taking the picture of notes after a meeting or a lecture allows you to listen during the meeting or lecture instead of writing notes.

- **Use your camera to take pictures of valuable information/documents in your life**

If you have any valuable piece of information that you can't afford to lose, use your camera to take its picture. That would serve as a backup in case of loss.

Tip: It is a good idea to back up your files/documents on cloud platforms like iCloud Drive, Dropbox, or Google Drive.

Connectivity

Windows Computer Connections

Your phone can be connected to a Windows computer with a USB cable. This will enable you to transfer files such as image files and video files to your Windows computer from your phone.

Warning: Do not disconnect the USB cable from a computer while the device is transferring or accessing the data. This may result in data loss.

Transferring content via USB

1. Connect your device to a Windows computer with an appropriate USB cable (like the one that came with your phone).

2. When prompted to allow access to phone data, tap **Allow.** If you don't choose Allow, your computer may not be able to access your phone.

3. Your device should appear in the same location where an external USB drive usually appears on your computer. Typically under "This PC/Computer" menu.

4. Open your device drive to see its folder. You may need to click on **Internal Storage** > **DCIM** > **100APPLE**. Note that you may not be able to access the folders if your phone is locked.

5. To transfer files from your phone to your computer, locate the file you want to transfer. Then press **Ctrl** + **C**. Go to the place where you want to paste it and press **Ctrl** + **V.**

6. Disconnect your phone just as you would disconnect an external memory drive. If you are using Windows 10, you may just remove the USB from the phone when you are done with the transfer. You may not need to click any disconnect icon before you remove your phone if you are using a Windows 10 PC.

Note: The process of file transfer described above is based on Windows 10 PC, if you are using Windows 7 or 8 PC, then there may be some differences.

Wi-Fi

Using your phone, you can connect to a wireless network.

To activate the Wi-Fi feature and connect to a network:

1. From the Home screen, tap **Settings** .
2. Tap **Wi-Fi**.
3. Tap the switch next to Wi-Fi to turn it on.

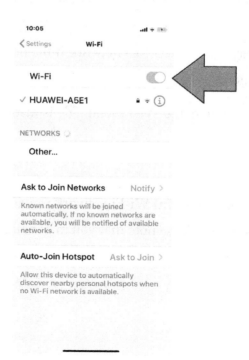

4. Your device then automatically scans for available networks and displays them.

5. Select a network.

6. Enter a password for the network (if needed) and tap **Join.**

7. To turn Wi-Fi off, from the Home screen, tap **Settings** > **Wi-Fi** and then tap the status switch. Alternatively, swipe down from the top-right edge of the screen and tap Wi-Fi icon .

Notes:

- The Wi-Fi feature running in the background will consume battery. To save battery, put it off whenever you are not using it.

- The Wi-Fi may not connect to a network if the network signal is not good.

- When Wi-Fi is active, the **Wi-Fi** icon is displayed on the status bar.

Tips:

To be notified when (an unknown) Wi-Fi network is available, turn on **Ask to Join Networks**. Please note that you may not get any announcement if you are already connected to a wireless network.

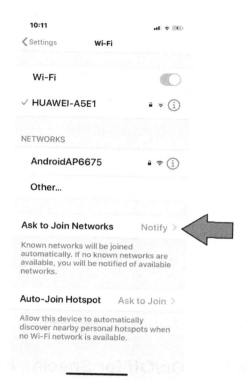

To adjust the settings for a particular Wi-Fi network, tap the info icon 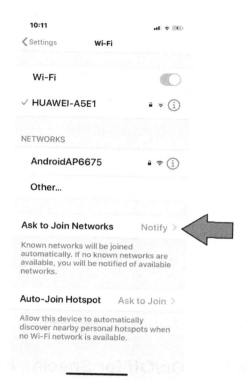 next to the Wi-Fi network. For example, to forget a network, just tap this info icon 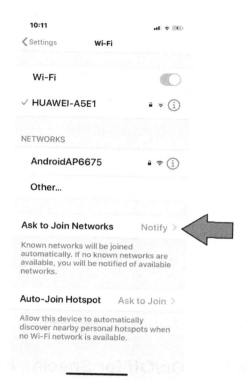 and tap **Forget This Network**. If you want apps on your iPhone to reduce their network data use when the selected network is in use, tap the status switch next to **Low Data Mode**.

Turning Mobile Data On/Off for Specific Apps

If you are very concerned about saving your data, you can prevent some apps from using your mobile data. In addition, turning off apps may help save battery life.

1. From the Home screen, tap **Settings** .
2. Tap **Cellular**.
3. Tap the status switch next to **Cellular Data** to enable this feature.

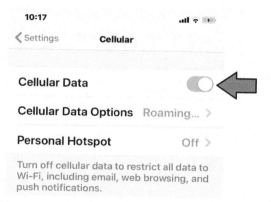

4. To prevent apps from accessing your mobile data, scroll down and tap the status switch next to the individual app.

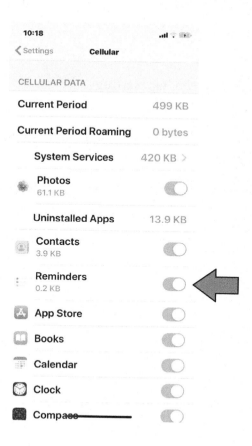

Depending on your network service provider, please note that the screenshot shown above may be different from the one on your device.

Tip: To quickly switch off cellular data, swipe down from the top-right edge of the screen and tap cellular data icon .

Using Your Phone as a Hotspot

If your network provider supports it, you can use this feature to share your mobile network with friends.

1. From the Home screen, tap **Settings** .
2. Tap **Cellular**.
3. Tap the status switch next to **Cellular Data** to turn it on.
4. Tap **Personal Hotspot**.
5. Tap the status switch next to **Allow Others to Join**. Please note that turning on Hotspot may disable Wi-Fi.

6. Read the on-screen connection instructions to know how to connect devices to your iPhone.

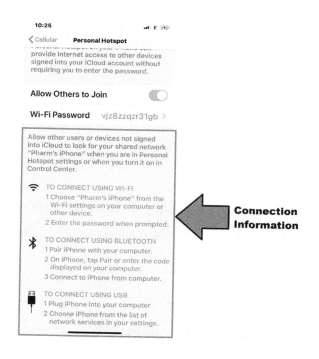

7. Tap the field next to **Wi-Fi Password** and enter a memorable password for your Personal Hotspot. Tap **Done**. This is the password that must be entered on other devices wishing to connect to your Personal Hotspot.

8. To change the name of your device, from the Home screen, tap **Settings**  > **General** > **About** > **Name**.

9. After enabling Personal Hotspot, your friends should be able to connect to it just like they connect to other wireless networks.

10. To turn off personal hotspot, from the Home screen, tap **Settings** 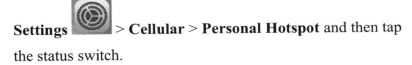 > **Cellular** > **Personal Hotspot** and then tap the status switch.

Access More Using Bluetooth

Bluetooth option allows you to connect to another Bluetooth device within range.

Note: If there are obstacles, the operating distance of the Bluetooth may be reduced. The Bluetooth communication range is usually around 33 feet.

To use the Bluetooth feature:

1. From the Home screen, tap **Settings** .

2. Tap **Bluetooth**.

3. Next to **Bluetooth**, tap the status switch.

4. Then Bluetooth automatically scans for nearby Bluetooth devices and displays them.

5. Tap a device to connect with. You may need to enter or accept a passcode. Tap **Pair**.

6. Pairing between two Bluetooth devices is usually a one-time process. Once two devices are paired, the devices continue to recognize this association and you may not need to re-enter a passcode.

7. To turn **Bluetooth** off, from the Home screen, tap **Settings** > **Bluetooth** and then tap the status switch. Alternatively, swipe down from the top-right edge of the screen and tap Bluetooth icon.

Unpairing a Paired Device

1. From the Home screen, tap **Settings**.
2. Tap **Bluetooth**.
3. Next to **Bluetooth**, tap the status switch.
4. Tap the info icon next to the paired device, and then tap **Forget This Device** to unpair the paired device. Select **Forget Device** when prompted.

Using the Airdrop

You can use Airdrop to send files between two Apple devices. To use this feature:

1. Swipe down from the top-right edge of the screen

2. Tap and hold the network card and select the Airdrop icon .

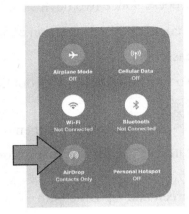

3. Select whom you like to receive file from.

4. To send a file, locate the file and select the share icon .

5. Select **Airdrop**.

6. Those people that can receive the file (within the range) will be listed. The person that wants to receive the file must turn on his/her Airdrop also.

7. On the recipient's phone, select **Accept**.

Location Services

Enabling location service allows Map and other apps to serve you content related services.

To activate location services:

1. From the Home screen, tap **Settings** 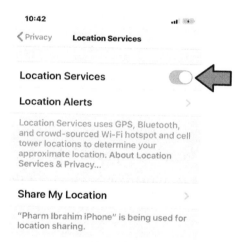.
2. Scroll down and tap **Privacy**.
3. Tap **Location Services**.
4. Tap the status switch next to the **Location Services**.

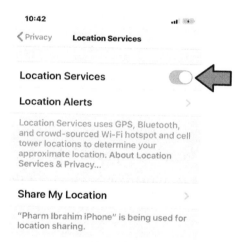

5. To prevent apps from accessing your location, tap the individual app under **Share My Location** and choose **Never**.

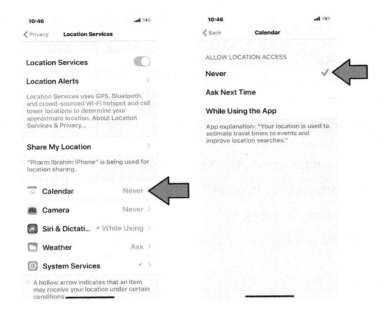

Find My iPhone

You can use this feature to locate your phone if lost.

Note: Find My iPhone must be turned on before your iPhone is lost. To do this:

1. From the Home screen, tap **Settings** .
2. Tap on your account name (in this case, it is **Pharm Ibrahim**).

3. Tap **Find My**.

4. Tap **Find My iPhone** and make sure the status switch is switched on. Also, if you want Apple to note the last location of your phone when the battery is critically low, enable the status switch next to **Send Last Location**. Make sure **Enable Offline Finding** is also enabled.

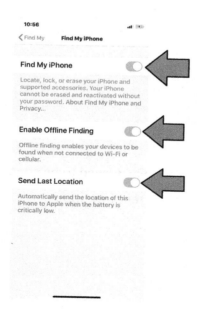

To find you lost phone:

1. Open a web browser and go to **https://www.icloud.com/find**

2. Enter your Apple ID and password. Then click the small arrow icon.

3. If necessary, click **Find My iPhone.**

4. Click **All Devices** and click your phone name. Your iPhone's current location will be displayed on the map. You can also select other options like erasing your iPhone, turning on lost mode, or ringing your phone. **Lost mode** allows you to display a phone number on the phone so that people can reach you using that phone number. To activate lost mode, simply click on **Lost Mode** and follow the prompts.

Please note that your lost phone may need to be connected to the internet for you to access its current location.

Settings

Settings menu give you the opportunity to customize your device as you like.

To access the settings menu:

1. From the Home screen, tap **Settings** .
2. Tap a setting category.

Search for Settings

It is advisable to use the searching feature when you are not sure exactly where to find a certain setting.

1. From the Home screen, tap **Settings** .
2. Swipe down if needed and tap **Search**.

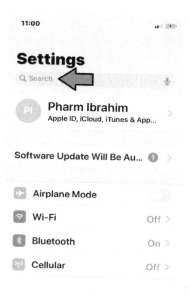

3. Enter a search phrase in the Search field. The list filters as you write.

4. Tap an option (make sure you select the best match).

Hint: There is a tip to getting what you want from your device. From time to time, you will want to customize your phone specially. All you need to do in a period like this is to open the Settings as described above. Then tap the Search tab and enter a search word relating to what you want to do.

What You Must Know About iPhone 11 or iPhone 11 Pro/Pro Max

How To Find Your Phone When Lost

As a human being, it is not impossible that you may misplace your phone. If someone else (a thief) has not taken custody of it, there are steps to follow to find it. These steps have been discussed at length in page 222 to 224; please refer to it for details.

How To Reduce Your Mobile Data Usage on iPhone 11 or iPhone 11 Pro/Pro Max

If you realize that you are using more MB/Data than normal, there are steps to follow to reduce your data consumption.

1. The first thing is to make sure that you update apps on Wi-Fi only. You can configure this by going to the settings under the individual app.

2. Monitor/limit your cellular data usage: To do this, please go to the page 214-216. In addition, there are many applications on Apple store allowing you to monitor your data usage. Knowing how you use your data will enable you to figure out what to do.

How to Conserve iPhone 11, iPhone 11 Pro, or iPhone 11 Pro Max Battery Life

If you use your phone heavily, you may notice that you have to charge iPhone 11, iPhone 11 Pro, or iPhone 11 Pro Max twice a day in order to keep the phone on. There are steps to follow to ensure that your phone serves you throughout the day with just a single charge.

1. **Reduce the screen brightness:** I have realized over time that screen brightness consumes a lot of energy. There is usually a substantial difference between using a phone with maximum brightness and using it with moderate brightness. As a rule, don't use your phone with maximum brightness unless you can't see what is on the screen clearly. For example, if you are outdoor. And please make sure you reduce it immediately when it is no more needed. To reduce the screen brightness, tap **Settings** > **Display & Brightness**. Then use the slider under **BRIGHTNESS** to adjust the screen brightness. To automatically adapt your iPhone display based on ambient lighting conditions, make sure the status switch next to **True Tone** is enabled.

2. **Shorten the Screen timeout:** If you really want to save your battery, you must try to shorten the screen timeout. Reducing how long your phone will stay lit up after you finish

interacting with it will really help you to save battery. To

manage the screen timeout settings, tap **Settings** >

Display & Brightness > Auto-Lock and choose an option.

3. **Turn off Wi-Fi and Bluetooth:** When you are not using Wi-Fi or Bluetooth, please always remember to put them off. These features really consume energy and they are better off when not in use.

4. **Use a good charger:** Using a bad charger can endanger the health of your phone/battery, and it is better to avoid such practice.

5. **Consider switching off your phone:** If you are not going to use your phone for an extended period, you may consider switching off your phone.

6. **Use headphones:** Using the headphones is another cool way to save your battery. Extended use of audio speakers of your phone may drain your battery faster.

How to Take Screenshot on Your iPhone

Another task you can perform on your device is taking a screenshot. To take a screenshot with your device, please follow the instructions below:

While at the exact screen you want to capture, press and hold the Side key and the volume up button simultaneously. You should hear a short sound when the screenshot is captured if your phone is not in Silent mode. You can view captured images in **Photos** app.

Extras

What You Must Do Before Selling or Giving away Your iPhone 11, iPhone 11 Pro, or iPhone 11 Pro Max

Please if you are planning to sell or give away your iPhone, make sure you completely erase your data on it.

To completely erase your data:

1. From the Home screen, tap **Settings** .

2. Tap on your account name (in this case, it is **Pharm Ibrahim**).

3. Scroll down and tap **Sign Out**. Tap **Sign Out** again when prompted. To back up your information before you sign out, tap **iCloud** > **iCloud Backup** > **Back Up Now**.

4. Then go back to **Settings** .

5. Tap **General**.

6. Tap **Reset**.

7. Tap **Erase All Content and Settings.** If prompted to enter your Apple ID and password, enter it.

8. Tap **Erase iPhone** and follow the prompts to complete the erasing process.

Please note that if you decide not to sell your iPhone again, you will need to set it up all over again. In addition, features like **Find My iPhone** may be turned off when you perform a complete reset.

Traveling with Your Phone—What to Know

While traveling abroad with your iPhone, there are a few things to know. These things are discussed below.

1. Unlock your phone and plan to get a local SIM card

If you are traveling abroad, it is important you consider unlocking your phone to use foreign SIM cards on your phone. Generally, you can unlock your phone by contacting your network service provider. If your phone is already unlocked, then have a clear plan to get a local SIM card when you get to your destination. Generally, using a local SIM card for your calls will save your money than roaming. **Note**: If you are unable to unlock your phone and you want to stay several months abroad, consider buying a cheap unlocked phone.

2. Get to know about roaming

If you are not planning to unlock your phone or get a local SIM card, then I would recommend that you know about the roaming plans of your network service provider. You can easily do this by contacting your network service provider.

3. Set up a lock screen

It is important to set up a lock screen while going abroad. This would save you a lot of stress if you misplace the phone. Security in some places in the world is bad and your phone can easily be snatched from you. Even if your phone is not stolen, you can misplace your phone while moving from one place to another. If you have set up a screen lock, you can be sure that it would be extremely hard (if not impossible) for people to access your data on the lost phone. To know how to set up a lock screen, see page 51.

Tip: If you mistakenly misplace your phone, you may locate it by following the steps under **Find My iPhone** (see page 222-224).

4. Get a power bank (USB Battery Pack)

Charging your phone might not be easy while abroad. I would advise you to consider getting a power bank to charge your phone. You can get a cheap and reliable power bank from Amazon.

5. Monitor and save your data

Data are quite expensive in some countries of the world. I would advise you to monitor and save data as much as you can. To know how to save data on your phone, see page 227.

6. Be careful when using Wireless network

Using a wireless network in a foreign country demands extra care. There are some countries that are notorious for hacking. I would recommend you research any country you are visiting to know how best to prepare. To learn how to stay secured when connected to a wireless network, see page 236.

7. Get familiar with Google Translate

If the country you are visiting does not speak your language, then you need someone or something to help you with language translation. Interestingly, Google Translate might provide some help in this regard. To start using Google Translate, visit **https://translate.google.com**

8. Get familiar with the Map application

The Map app on your phone can help you navigate from one place to another. You can easily know the route to your destination using this app. I would advise you familiarize yourself with the Map app before traveling. This application can save you a lot of stress and time.

Using Guided Access to Restrict the Access of Your Child When Using Your Phone

If you want your child to be confined to just a single app when you give him/her your phone, then activate Guided Access.

Guided Access keeps your iPhone in a single app, and allows you to control which features are available.

To enable Guided Access:

1. Go to **Settings** .
2. Tap **Accessibility**.
3. Scroll down and tap **Guided Access**.
4. Then tap the status switch next to **Guided Access** to activate this feature.
5. To set the passcode to be used when Guided Access is active, tap on **Passcode Settings** and then select **Set Guided Access Passcode**. Then follow the prompts.

Managing Guided Access

1. To activate Guided Access after you have enabled it, triple-click the side button in the app you want to use.
2. Select **Guided Access** if prompted.
3. If there is any part of the screen/app you want to disable, simply circle it.
4. Tap **Start** (found at the top of the screen) and enter your Guided Access passcode if needed.
5. To exit Guided Access, triple-click the side button again and enter your Guided Access passcode.
6. Select **End** at the top of the screen.

Safety Precautions When Using iPhone 11, iPhone 11 Pro, or iPhone 11 Pro Max on Wi-Fi

With many free Wi-Fi hotspots, it is likely that you are going to find yourself using Wi-Fi more on your phone. There are a few things to keep in mind when using Wi-Fi.

1. Confirm the Network Name

Hackers sometimes set up a fake Wi-Fi network in order to tap into the information of unwitting public users. To avoid this, make sure you are sure of the name of the network you are connecting to. You may ask any trusted individual around you if you doubt the name of a network.

2. Connect to a Secured Site

Whenever you are sending sensitive information, always make sure that the site is a secured website. You can know whether a website is a secured site or not by checking whether the URL address of the website starts with **HTTPS.** If it starts with https, then it should be a secured site.

3. Get a Virtual Private Network (VPN)

It is highly important you use a virtual private network when using a public network. There are both free and paid VPN providers.

4. Avoid Automatic Connection

Make sure your Wi-Fi is off when not using it to avoid your phone automatically connecting to an open network. Turning your Wi-Fi off when not using it will also save your battery.

I am Having a Dwindling Love for My iPhone 11, iPhone 11 Pro, or iPhone 11 Pro Max; What Should I do?

It is possible that after buying iPhone 11, iPhone 11 Pro, or iPhone 11 Pro Max, you realize that it performs below your expectations. It is likely that you dislike your phone because of its hardware or software issue. Generally, the hardware has to do with the design, the phone make-up, the weight of the phone, etc., while the software has to do with OS and applications.

If your love for iPhone 11, iPhone 11 Pro, or iPhone 11 Pro Max is reducing because of the software, there is a way out. You can take time to look for beneficial apps to install on your device.

If your love for iPhone 11, iPhone 11 Pro, or iPhone 11 Pro Max is reducing because of the hardware then it is either you learn how to live with it (you may have to force yourself to love it) or you sell it. If you are considering selling your phone, then make sure you read the previous section (see page 231 to 232) before selling it.

Troubleshooting

If the touch screen responds slowly or improperly or your phone is not responding, try the following:

- Remove any protective covers (screen protector) from the touch screen.
- Ensure that your hands are clean and dry when tapping.
- Press the power button once to lock the screen and press it again to unlock the screen and enter your passcode if required.
- Switch off your device and turn it on again.

Your Phone Doesn't Charge

- Make sure you are using the recommended Apple charger to charge your phone.
- If the iPhone 11, iPhone 11 Pro, or iPhone 11 Pro Max does not indicate that it is charging, unplug the power adapter, switch off your phone and switch it on again.
- Make sure you are using the USB cable that came with the iPhone 11, iPhone 11 Pro, or iPhone 11 Pro Max or anyone that has similar specs.

Your device is hot to the touch

When you use applications that require more power or use applications on your device for an extended period of time, your phone may be a bit hot to touch. This is normal, and it should not affect performance. You may just allow your phone to rest for some time or close some applications.

Your phone freezes or has a fatal error

If your phone freezes or it is unresponsive and refuses to power off, press and release the volume up button, press and release the volume down button and then press and hold the side button until your mobile phone restarts.

Phone does not have cellular data network

Make sure you don't have limited network connectivity in that area. If your network is good and you still don't have cellular network, then make sure the Airplane mode is off. To check whether Airplane mode is enabled, swipe down from the top-right edge of the screen. The Airplane mode icon will appear colored when enabled/on. Please note that the Airplane mode should be disabled/off to access cellular networks.

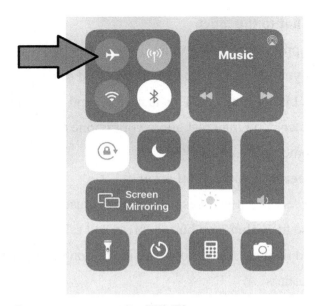

The phone does not connect to Wi-Fi

- Try restarting the Wi-Fi.

- Move closer to your router, turn off and turn on Wi-Fi again.

- Restart your router and modem. Unplug the modem and router for few minutes and plug the modem in and then the router.

- Try restarting your phone.

Another Bluetooth device is not located

- Ensure Bluetooth feature is activated on your phone and the device you want to connect to.

- Ensure that your phone and the other Bluetooth device are within the maximum Bluetooth range (within 33 feet).

A connection is not established when you connect your phone to a PC

- Ensure that the USB cable you are using is compatible with your device.

- Ensure that you have the proper drivers/apps installed and updated on your PC.

Audio quality is poor

- When you are in an area with weak or poor reception, you may lose reception. Try moving to another area and then try again.

Phone does not ring out

- Press/Slide the silent/ring button.

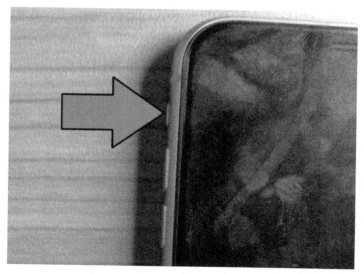

- Check if Do Not Disturb (see page 185) is enabled. If Do Not Disturb is enabled, your phone may not ring out.

Safety Precautions

A. To prevent electric shock, fire, and explosion:
1. Do not use damaged power cords or plugs, or loose electrical sockets.
2. Do not touch the power cord with a wet hand.
3. Do not bend or damage the power cord.
4. Do not short-circuit the charger.
5. Do not use your phone during a thunderstorm.
6. Do not dispose of your phone by putting it in fire.

B. Follow all safety warnings and regulations when using your device in restricted areas.

C. Comply with all safety warnings and regulations regarding mobile device usage while operating a vehicle.

D. Proper care and use of your phone
1. Do not use or store your phone in hot or cold areas. It is recommended to use your device at a temperature from 5^0C to 35^0C.
2. Do not put your phone near magnetic fields.
3. Do not use your camera flash close to eyes of people or pets because it can cause temporary loss of vision or damage the eyes.
4. Avoid disturbing others when using your phone in public.
5. Keep your phone away from small children because they may mistakenly damage it. It may look like a toy to them.

Just Before You Go (Please Read!)

Although I have put in tremendous efforts into writing this guide, I am confident that I have not said it all.

I have no doubt believing that I have not written everything possible about this device.

Therefore, I want you to do me a favor.

If you will like to know how to perform a task that is not included in this guide, please let me know by sending me an email at **pharmibrahimguides@gmail.com**. I will try as much as possible to reply you as soon as I can.

You may also visit my author's page at

www.amazon.com/author/pharmibrahim

And please don't forget to follow me when you visit my author's page, just click or tap on **Follow** button located below the profile picture.

Index